Parliamentary Procedure: a programmed introduction

Revised Edition

john w. gray
University of Arkansas at Little Rock

richard g. rea
University of Arkansas at Fayetteville

Scott, Foresman and Company
Glenview, Illinois   Brighton, England

Preface

Over 2000 years ago Socrates laid the foundation for programmed learning in his method of teaching through dialog. Later, the great Roman teacher Quintilian defined the educational process as a "series of arranged victories." Sidney L. Pressey dusted off this idea and pointed the way toward what is today called "programmed learning."

The use of improved methods of instruction has become essential in these days of crowded classrooms and intellectually demanding curricula. Programmed learning through a programmed text is one such method. The programmed text leads the student to understanding by a series of very small steps. It allows him to proceed at his own pace and provides him with immediate reinforcement of correct responses. Proceeding through the sequence of small steps, the student knows the required responses; he does not have to guess. Checking immediately against the printed responses, he is rewarded, achieving the "victories" of which Quintilian spoke, and his knowledge is reinforced.

This programmed text is an introduction to the basic core knowledge of parliamentary procedure. Complete and detailed information about all aspects of the subject can be found in an authoritative parliamentary procedure manual, such as *Robert's Rules of Order Newly Revised* (1970). You are encouraged to consult a source such as this one whenever questions arise about the more intricate aspects of the subject. We hope, however, that the material programmed in this text will enable you, as a student of parliamentary procedure, to become a better member of an organization, to conduct meetings proficiently, and to participate more effectively in group process.

This text is divided into ten sets of frames. Set A, Introduction, presents a synoptic view of the origin and use of parliamentary procedure. Set B deals exclusively with the problems of conducting a meeting and the steps in the order of business. Sets C and D are devoted to the methods of making and amending a motion, with emphasis on the method of gaining the floor and voting procedures. Sets E, F, G, and H classify each commonly used motion, giving its usage and its precedence in relation to the other motions. Set I discusses the essential officers of an organization and the qualifications and responsibilities for each office; procedure for election of officers is included in this set. Finally, Set J describes how to draw up a constitution and by-laws in organizing a club.

We are convinced that parliamentary procedure cannot be learned from a textbook only. You must have an opportunity to apply the procedures in practice and under supervision. Through the use of *Parliamentary Procedure: A Programmed Introduction, Revised Edition* as a self-instructional device, valuable classroom time can be reserved for just such supervised practice.

Throughout the program, the term *chairman* is used to name the presiding officer of an organization. Likewise, the use of the masculine form of the third person pronoun is prevalent throughout the book (for example, ". . . when a member wishes to speak, *he* must first address the chair"). We wish to explain that these wordings are merely devices to simplify the language of the program. By these terms, we include all members of an organization, regardless of sex.

This program was originally tested at Auburn University and Louisiana State University, and thanks are extended to the speech departments of these universities. The original edition of *Parliamentary Procedure: A Programmed Introduction* was used successfully at colleges and universities all over the country, as well as in many clubs and organizations of widely varying types. The authors are grateful for the assistance of a grant-in-aid from Auburn University to carry out the original research, testing, and development of this text. Finally, we express our gratitude to the many students for their evaluation and testing of the program, and to our wives for their constant faith and enthusiasm.

J.W.G.
R.G.R.

A BASIC PHILOSOPHY OF PARLIAMENTARY PROCEDURE

Most organizations in American society were started by people of good will, people who made every effort to see that the group served all its members. In order to achieve this objective it was necessary to have a consistent set of rules to govern its actions. This was the spirit in which Thomas Jefferson prepared his parliamentary manual. Jefferson felt a need for uniformity of proceedings in business meetings and stated his belief that "It is very material that order, decency and regularity be preserved in a dignified public body." In this way, parliamentary procedure became "democracy in miniature" for both public and private organizations in America.

There are many manuals on parliamentary procedure available to you and your organization. Most of them are similar in the rules they present. If you learn the procedure from one good manual, there is no reason to fear that your procedure might not be applicable to any group you join. The rules and procedures found in these manuals should be adapted to the needs and desires of the members of the organization using them. A safe rule- of- thumb is to use no more of the rules than is necessary and desired by the members of your organization. If your business meetings are being carried on without undue controversy, without a waste of time and group effort, and without confusion over procedure, then you are probably using the best procedure available for your organization, regardless of whether or not you are using the exact procedure outlined and provided in the parliamentary procedure manuals.

Parliamentary procedure was not devised as an orderly method for conducting problem-solving discussions. The rules were designed as an orderly procedure for making and recording decisions in business meetings. It is true that parliamentary procedure provides for a certain amount of debate and discussion but it also often discourages discussion and debate (i.e. Limit Debate, Object to consideration, Refer to a Committee, etc.). There are many people today who are suspicious of the value of parliamentary procedure due to its frequent use in groups whose purpose is problem solving and where group discussion might serve as a better method for conducting the meeting. If the committees of an organization operate properly and take their jobs seriously, there will be less need for argument and debate in business meetings. It is the duty of the committees to research and discuss the matters referred to them and to make recommendations to the organization concerning possible actions which might be desirable. A majority of the problem-solving activities are carried out by the committees before the business meeting is called, and through the officers and committees the members are provided with the information needed to make intelligent decisions.

Most violent controversies and misunderstandings in groups arise either from lack of information or from suspicion. Both of these ills might easily be relieved or avoided by providing the members, far in advance of the meeting, with all pertinent facts, so that they can study them before the deliberations start. It is very difficult and disconcerting for an intelligent individual to arrive at a meeting totally unprepared to make rational and mature decisions. Often a person deeply conscientious about his actions will either fail to vote, create controversy, or rebel altogether when faced with making decisions without the proper information. Those persons less conscientious but extremely suspicious might have the same reaction. It might be helpful to prepare a detailed agenda for each meeting and to place a copy of this agenda in the hands of all members in advance of the meeting. The agenda could include a listing of all items of business to come before the group and explanations of those items that might be controversial or misunderstood, a list of all committees whose reports are due (and the name of the committee chairman and members), reminders of actions taken at the last meeting, etc. It seems that such an agenda would not only create interest but also would promote attendance and act as a good promotional document for the organization. Anyone seeing it would realize that the group was active and working. A committee chairman, after seeing his name on the agenda, might have a renewed interest in carrying out his duties and in being in attendance to give his report. Members of a committee who know that the committee has been negligent in their work might be encouraged to seek out the committee chairman and see that their report was prepared and that they were well represented in the meeting.

And finally, it is impossible to overstress the necessity of training the organization in the use of parliamentary procedure. This training process must include not only practice in the procedure's actual techniques but it must also encourage a respect for the rules and provide for a study of the philosophy behind the procedure.

The Authors

Contents

INSTRUCTIONS

This textbook is designed to teach basic parliamentary procedure by means of a self-teaching device, a *program*. The program is divided into ten sets; each set treats a different aspect of parliamentary procedure. The program is intended to be taken in its entirety, beginning with Set A and continuing through to the end of Set J. However, each set is fairly complete unto itself, and you may take any one set by itself if your purpose is only to review one facet of parliamentary procedure.

Each set is composed of numbered frames. You must start with the first frame and proceed through the set in sequence or you will find that your knowledge of the subject matter is incomplete, for the program is based on the principle of acquiring knowledge and comprehension in small increments.

Use a card or piece of paper (3″ x 5″ index card is ideal) to expose one frame at a time. Read the frame carefully. Note the italicized words and phrases; they are aids in completing many of the frames. In each frame there are blanks when you are required to make a *response*. The number of blanks in the frame indicates the number of words in the desired response. Write the missing word or words in the space at the right of the frame. *Do not fill in the blanks in the frame.* After you have completed your response, move the card down to expose the next frame. As you do so, you will also expose the answer to the previous frame, which is given in the right-hand column opposite the beginning of the next frame. Check your answer before proceeding to the next frame. If your answer is incorrect, go back and review the previous few frames before proceeding with the program. If your answer is correct, proceed with the next frame. Try to complete as much of the program as possible at one sitting.

In order to be sure that you understand the procedure just outlined, here is an example.

1. This textbook teaches the basics of parliamentary procedure by means of a *program*. A self-teaching device which presents information in small segments is called a _____ .

2. This program is divided into frames; in each frame you are required to make a *response*.   *program*

The number of blanks in each frame indicates the number of words in the desired _____ .

3. Write your response to the right of each frame. Then check your answer against the correct response which is given in the right-hand column opposite the beginning of the next _____ .

response

4. If your answer is correct, proceed to the next _____ of the program.

frame

Now you are ready to begin the program.

frame

set A

INTRODUCTION

Place a card or piece of paper (approximately 3" x 5") over the page. Move the card down the page to expose one frame at a time. Read the frame carefully. The blanks in the frame indicate where essential information is missing; the number of blanks indicates the number of words in the desired response. Do not write in the blanks; write your response in the space to the right of the frame. Then move the card down to expose the next frame; as you do so you will also expose the correct answer to the previous frame, which is given in the right-hand column opposite the next frame. Check your answer before continuing the program.

A 1.   Our democracy is based on government by public opinion, which is guaranteed expression by our freedom of speech. The privilege of expressing ourselves in public and in private on any issue is called ____ ____ ____.

A 2.   In addition to freedom of speech, we also have a responsibility to our fellow citizen not to hinder him in exercising the same ____ ____ ____.

freedom of speech

A 3.   We usually exercise freedom of speech in public gatherings (club meetings, conventions, etc.) where we have the opportunity to *speak* as well as to ____ to what the other people have to say.

freedom of speech

A 4.   The best system of rules yet devised for making and recording decisions within a group is called parliamentary procedure. These rules provide an opportunity to exercise freedom of _____ .

listen

A 5.   The term *parliamentary procedure* comes from the British governing body called the _____ .

speech

A 6.   The British Parliament developed a set of rules to keep order in their meetings. This set of rules was called _____ _____ .

Parliament

A 7.   When the colonies were organized in America, they also needed rules for governing their meetings. They devised their own rules but still called these rules _____ _____ .

parliamentary procedure

A 8.   The term *parliamentary procedure* comes from the _____ Parliament.

parliamentary procedure

A 9.   Parliamentary procedure guarantees that each individual has an opportunity to speak. When the time comes to stand up and be heard, _____ procedure provides the opportunity.

British

A 10.   The best system man has discovered for keeping order and giving each person the chance to be heard in business meetings is called _____ _____ .

parliamentary

A 11.   Order can be maintained in a meeting by using parliamentary procedure. If, for example, the members of a large organization are engaged in a debate, equal control is placed on all members to assure proper debate through _____ _____ .

parliamentary procedure

A 12.   If a group consists of only a few members, it is less likely that ___ ___ will be needed to maintain order.

parliamentary procedure

A 13.   The nature and purpose of a group's meeting will aid in determining whether or not ___ ___ should be used.

parliamentary procedure

A 14.   If a group is trying to arrive at an answer acceptable to all of its members, then *group discussion* should be employed. Through ___ ___, consensus (agreement by all) can be attained.

parliamentary procedure

A 15.   If the purpose of the group is to arrive at a solution in a very short time, then ___ ___ can be used to determine the will of the majority of the members.

group discussion

A 16.   If a group has unlimited time to decide on a solution and it is desirable for all members to participate in making the decision, then ___ ___ should be used in order to gain consensus.

parliamentary procedure

A 17.   Parliamentary procedure protects the *minority* group in a meeting by giving those members an equal chance to voice their opinions. Therefore, parliamentary procedure not only determines the will of the majority but also protects the rights of the ___.

group discussion

A 18. Within a group using ___ procedure, each member's vote has equal significance.

minority

A 19.   A member's *vote* has as much significance as an officer's ___ when parliamentary procedure is used.

parliamentary procedure

A 20. Parliamentary procedure guarantees that each member will have an equal right to voice his opinion on a subject and an equal _____ in determining what the organization will do about each subject discussed.

vote

A 21. Parliamentary procedure provides for free discussion of all subjects but limits the discussion to one *subject* at a time. One subject must be disposed of before another _____ can be introduced.

vote

A 22.   One of the best ways to maintain order in a business meeting is to use the rules provided in the system called _____ _____.

subject

A 23. Parliamentary procedure might be compared with our traffic laws. The traffic laws tell us when to *stop*, and parliamentary procedure tells us when to be *silent*. The traffic laws tell us when to *go*, and parliamentary procedure tells us when to _____.

parliamentary procedure

A 24. Without parliamentary procedure, we often find ourselves "running into one another"—speaking at the same time. Parliamentary procedure will help "direct our traffic" and prevent our speaking at the same _____.

speak or talk

A 25.   Traffic laws are designed to serve a certain group of people. In the same way, parliamentary procedure must be molded to fit the needs of the members of the _____ using it.

time

A 26. It should be kept in mind that laws (rules) are for people and not _____ for laws.

group, organization, club, etc.

A 27. Parliamentary procedure will never be the same for all *organizations.* If the members

people

use parliamentary procedure, then it must be molded to fit the needs of the _____.

A 28. The United States Steel Corporation would not use the same procedure in its meetings as would the local Lions Club. Parliamentary procedure will never be the same for all _____.

organization

A 29. The idea is to make parliamentary procedure work for the organization and its members. It is necessary for each member to understand the basic rules involved so that he may participate in his organization's business _____.

organizations

A 30. Many times individuals fail to participate in the discussion at a meeting because they do not know the *procedure* being used. Each person will be a more productive member if he learns the _____ and joins in the discussion.

meetings

A 31. With a knowledge of the basic rules of _____ _____, an individual can freely participate in business meetings and feel as if he is receiving the full advantage of his _____ _____ _____.

procedure or rules

A 32. Each *citizen* in our democracy should exercise his freedom of speech, but he must exercise it responsibly. Our organizations, like our democracy, must be composed of responsible _____.

parliamentary procedure · freedom of speech

You are now ready to begin Set B, Conducting a Meeting.

citizens

set B

CONDUCTING A MEETING[1]

Place a card or piece of paper (approximately 3″ x 5″) over the page. Move the card down the page to expose one frame at a time. Read the frame carefully. The blanks in the frame indicate where essential information is missing; the number of blanks indicates the number of words in the desired response. Do not write in the blanks; write your response in the space to the right of the frame. Then move the card down to expose the next frame; as you do so you will also expose the correct answer to the previous frame, which is given in the right-hand column opposite the next frame. Check your answer before continuing the program.

B 1. To avoid *confusion* in business meetings, the members normally follow a definite order of business which is composed of eight steps to be followed from the beginning to the end of the meeting. By using these steps, _____ can be avoided in meetings.

B 2. The order of business could be compared with the instructions of a do-it-yourself kit in which the different *steps* are numbered in sequence. The order of business is usually composed of eight _____ to be followed during the meeting.

confusion

B 3. The order of business is composed of _____ steps.

steps

[1] For a more detailed discussion of this subject, see *Robert's Rules of Order Newly Revised*, page 300.

B 4. This pattern of eight steps is called the _____ of _____.

eight

B 5. The meeting should begin with step number _____ and end with step number _____.

order · business

B 6. In molding parliamentary procedure to best serve the needs of a _____, it may be necessary to change the order and/or the number of steps in the order of business.

one · eight

B 7. The first step in the order of business is the *call to order.* At the appointed time for the meeting to start, the chairman will _____ the meeting to _____.

group

B 8. The chairman calls the meeting to order by saying, "The meeting will please come to order." This is the _____ step in the order of business.

call · order

B 9. If the club meets on Thursday at 7:00 p.m., then at that time the chairman will _____ the meeting _____ _____.

first

B 10. The order of business has _____ steps, and the first one is the _____ _____ _____.

call · to order

B 11. Some organizations have an invocation and roll call after the _____ to _____, but this practice is optional and is not considered one of the eight steps in the order of business.

eight · call to order

B 12. If an organization wishes to begin its meetings with an invocation, the invocation should be included after the call to order but before the _____ of _____.

call · order

B 13. The roll call is necessary to determine

order · business

if a *quorum* is present. A _____ is determined
by calling the roll of the members to see if
enough members are present to carry out the
business of the organization. The _____ call is
optional for each organization.

B 14. The quorum of an organization is the
number of members that must be present in
order to carry out the _____ of the organization.

quorum · roll

B 15. Not all organizations have a roster of
members; if an organization does not have a
roster, then no _____ _____ could be taken.

business

B 16. When a roll call is taken to determine
whether or not a quorum is present, the quorum is based upon the *number* present at a
meeting and not the _____ voting.

roll call

B 17. If a quorum is necessary in order to
conduct business, a _____ _____ is taken to
determine the number of members present.

number

B 18. The second step in the order of business is the *reading and approval of the minutes.*
The chairman will say, "The secretary will
please read the _____ of the last meeting."

roll call

B 19. At the time the meeting is to start, the
chairman will call the meeting to _____ and
then have the secretary read the _____ of the
last meeting.

minutes

B 20. The minutes of the last meeting are a
record of what business took place at the previous meeting. The reading and approval of
the minutes is the _____ step in the order of
business.

order · minutes

B 21.   The purpose of having the minutes read and approved is to recall to the members what was accomplished at the last ____.

second

B 22.   If the members agree that the minutes read are a true account of the last meeting, then the minutes are *approved.* The secretary will write the word "____" at the end of the minutes along with the date and his signature.

meeting

B 23.   If a member finds fault with the minutes, he may correct them by addressing the chair and stating his objections. After the corrections have been made, the secretary writes "____" at the end of the minutes along with the date and his ____.

approved

B 24.   Once the minutes have been read and approved by the organization, they become a permanent record of all business discussed and all action taken by the ____.

approved · signature

B 25.   The third step in the order of business consists of the *reports of standing committees.* The standing committees are the permanent committees of the organization. After the reading and approval of the minutes, the next step in the order of business is the ____ ____ ____ ____.

organization

B 26.   The standing committees are the ____ committees of an organization.

reports of standing committees

B 27.   Examples of standing committees could be: the finance committee, the membership committee, the public relations committee, etc. The reports from these committees constitute the ____ step in the order of business.

permanent

B 28. A report from a standing committee is generally read by the chairman of that committee. The *order* in which the reports of standing committees are given is usually dictated by the _____ in which the standing committees appear in the constitution.

third

B 29. The fourth step in the order of business consists of the *reports of special committees.* The *special* committees are only temporary committees which are set up to investigate _____ problems of the organization.

order

B 30. Examples of special committees could be: awards committee, nominating committee, centennial committee, etc. Reports from these committees constitute the _____ step of the order of business.

special

B 31. The fourth step in the order of business consists of the _____ _____ _____ _____.

fourth

B 32. These special committees are not *permanent* committees but _____ committees.

reports of special committees

B 33. So far we have studied four of the eight steps in the order of business. Fill in the missing steps:
1. call to order
2.
3. reports of standing committees
4.

temporary

B 34. Fill in the missing steps in the order of business:
1.
2. reading and approval of the minutes
3.
4. reports of special committees

2) reading and approval of the minutes 4) reports of special committees

B 35.   List the first *four* steps in the order of business.

1) call to order
3) reports of standing committees

B 36.   The fifth step in the order of business is *unfinished business.* By "unfinished business" we mean any business left over from a previous _____.

1) call to order
2) reading and approval of the minutes
3) reports of standing committees
4) reports of special committees

B 37.   If the business was not finished at the last meeting, it must be brought before the group again. This unsettled business is known as _____ _____.

meeting

B 38.   Bringing unfinished business up before the organization is the _____ step in the order of business.

unfinished (or old) business

B 39.   It is the duty of the chairman to see that all unfinished business is presented to the organization at the next _____.

fifth

B 40.   The sixth step in the order of business is *new business.* If a member wishes to propose something new, he must do it under the sixth step which is _____ _____.

meeting

B 41.   New business consists of anything that has not been brought before the club at a previous meeting. If a member wants to propose that the club purchase an adding machine and this idea has not been mentioned before, he will bring it up under _____ _____.

new business

B 42.   Under the heading of new business, as anywhere else in the order of business, only one subject (motion) can be considered at a time. If a member wishes to propose new business to the club, he will do it under step number _____ of the order of business.

new business

B 43.   Because of the large amount of fresh
and recent information available to progres-
sive organizations, more motions will probably
be made under the step called ____ ____ than
under any other step in the order of business.

six

B 44.   The seventh step in the order of business is *announcements.* When all of the new
motions have been disposed of under step
number six, then the floor is open for any
member to make an ____.

new business

B 45.   The chairman may receive announcements before the meeting. He will then present these under step number ____ of the
order of business.

announcement

B 46.   If a member wants to inform the organization of an item of interest to them, he
will make this statement under step number
seven of the order of business which is ____.

seven

B 47.   The eighth and last step in the order of
business is *adjournment.* When the business
has been completed, there must be a step provided to close the meeting. This step is called
____.

announcements

B 48.   When we adjourn, we close the ____.

adjournment

B 49.   Many clubs have a fixed time for end-
ing their meetings. If this fixed time is 9:00
p.m., then the club must ____ its meeting at
9:00 p.m.

meeting

B 50.   The eighth step in the order of business is ____.

adjourn or close

B 51.   We have seen how the order of busi-

adjournment

ness is organized into ＿＿ steps. These steps
are followed in order to avoid ＿＿ in the
meeting.

B 52.   Fill in the missing steps in the order of
business:
1. call to order
2.
3. reports of standing committees
4.
5. unfinished business
6. new business
7. announcements
8. adjournment

*eight · confusion,
disorder, etc.*

B 53.   Fill in the missing steps:
1.
2. reading and approval of the minutes
3.
4. reports of special committees
5. unfinished business
6.
7. announcements
8. adjournment

*2) reading and ap-
proval of the minutes
4) reports of special
committees*

B 54.   Now list *all eight* steps in the order of
business.

*1) call to order
3) reports of stand-
ing committees
6) new business*

You are now ready to begin Set C, Making a
Motion.

*1) call to order
2) reading and ap-
proval of the minutes
3) reports of stand-
ing committees
4) reports of special
committees 5) un-
finished business
6) new business
7) announcements
8) adjournment*

set C

MAKING A MOTION[1]

Place a card or piece of paper (approximately 3" x 5") over the page. Move the card down the page to expose one frame at a time. Read the frame carefully. The blanks in the frame indicate where essential information is missing; the number of blanks indicates the number of words in the desired response. Do not write in the blanks; write your response in the space to the right of the frame. Then move the card down to expose the next frame; as you do so you will also expose the correct answer to the previous frame, which is given in the right-hand column opposite the next frame. Check your answer before continuing the program.

C 1.   The person who conducts or presides over the meeting is called the *chairman.* During a business meeting the _____ will direct and regulate the activities.

C 2.   The chairman—or "chair" as he or she is sometimes called—presides over the business meetings of an _____.

chairman

C 3.   To be able to participate in a meeting, a member must gain the right to speak. The first step in gaining this right is to *address the chair.* Thus anytime a member wishes to speak in a meeting, he must first _____ the chair.

organization

[1] For a more detailed discussion of this subject, see *Robert's Rules of Order Newly Revised,* pages 23-47.

C 4.   Addressing the chair is very similar to a student's raising his hand in that both actions mean that someone's attention is being sought. When a member addresses the chair, he simply wants the chair's _____.

address

C 5.   The first step in gaining the right to speak in a business meeting is to _____ the chair.

attention

C 6.   A member addresses the chair by saying, "Mr. Chairman" or "Madam Chairman." When he has said this, the chairman knows that a member wishes to _____.

address

C 7.   After a member has addressed the chair, he must be *recognized* by the chair before he can speak. Thus the second step in gaining the right to speak is to await _____ from the chair.

speak

C 8.   The chair recognizes a member by saying, "The Chair recognizes Mr. . . ." If the member has addressed the chair by saying, "_____ _____," the chair will usually recognize him by saying, "_____ _____ _____ Mr. . . ."

recognition

C 9.   The chair would recognize Mr. John Doe by saying, "The Chair recognizes Mr. Doe." This would give Mr. Doe the right to _____.

Mr. Chairman · The Chair recognizes

C 10.   If Ms. Mary Smith has addressed the chair, she would know she had been recognized when the chair said, "_____ _____ _____ _____ _____."

speak

C 11.   Upon being recognized, a member has the *floor* or the right to speak. If you want

The Chair recognizes Ms. Smith

recognition, you must address the chair. If the
chair recognizes you, then you have the _____,
or the right to speak.

C 12.   Having the floor is the same as having
the _____ _____ _____.

floor

C 13.   The steps in gaining the floor or the
right to speak are:
1. address the _____
2. await _____ from the chair
3. rise and speak

right to speak

C 14.   You should now know how to gain the
floor in a business meeting. List (in your own
words) the *three* steps used in gaining the
floor.

chair · recognition

C 15.   If a member of an organization wishes
to propose any action (ask the group to do
something), he must state his proposal as a
motion. A clear but brief statement of a proposed action is called a _____.

1) address the chair
2) await recognition
from the chair
3) rise and speak

C 16.   If a member wants the organization to
do something such as make a purchase, dismiss a member, or give money to charity, he
would state this proposed action as a _____.

motion

C 17.   A motion that proposes some new action is sometimes called an *original main* _____.

motion

C 18.   When a person makes an original main
motion, he is proposing that the group take
some kind of _____ on a new item of business.

motion

C 19.   All business is brought before an organization by using the motion. Another

action

name for the motion proposing something
new is ____ ____ ____.

C 20.   Original main motions will hereafter
be referred to as simply main ____; other motions will be referred to by their specific
names.

original main motion

C 21.   Action is proposed in a business meeting by using what is commonly referred to as
a ____ ____.

motions

C 22.   A main motion may deal with any subject; therefore, if a member wants the group
to donate $10 to the Red Cross, he would
propose this action in a ____ ____.

main motion

C 23.   Main motions are recommendations to
an organization to take some definite ____.

main motion

C 24.   A main motion must be stated clearly
and simply so that all the members will ____
it.

action

C 25.   Main motions should be stated ____
and simply so that there is no misunderstanding.

understand

C 26.   The proper way to state a main motion
is to introduce it with the three words "*I
move that.*" If a member wishes to make a
main motion that the organization buy new
furniture, he would simply say, "____ ____
____ we buy new furniture."

clearly

C 27.   How would you make a motion to
paint the clubroom red? Write out your motion.

I move that

C 28.   How would you make a motion to
buy flame-resistant drapes for the clubroom?

*"I move that we
paint the clubroom
red."*

C 29.   As a member of an organization, you
wish to make a motion that the group give
$100 to charity. The procedure to follow
would be:
1. You must first ____ ____ ____.
2. The chair will then ____ you.
3. At this point you have the floor and will
state your main motion. Write out your
motion.

*"I move that we buy
flame-resistant
drapes for the club-
room."*

C 30.   Which of the following main motions
is/are well worded?
1. "Mr. Chairman, I move that this organization buy $500 worth of Savings Bonds."
2. "Mr. Chairman, I move that we definitely
consider giving some money to charity."

*1) address the chair
2) recognize 3) "I
move that we give
$100 to charity."*

C 31.   Again which of the following main
motions is/are well worded?
1. "I move that we give $50 to the Red
Cross."
2. "I move that we give some money to the
Community Chest."
3. "I move that we write all the people we can
think of and invite them to join our club."
4. "I move that we write all persons eligible
and invite them to join our club at the Janu-
ary meeting."
5. "I move that we give Henry all the money
he needs for his New York trip."

1

C 32.   Since you must gain the floor to make
a main motion, your first step is to ____ the
chair.

1 · 4

C 33.   The second step is to await ____ by
the chair.

address

C 34.   After you have been recognized, you may state your ___ ___.

recognition

C 35.   After a main motion has been made, a *second* is required to show that one other member approves of having the matter considered, and NOT necessarily that he approves of the motion itself. A person seconds a motion by simply saying, "I ___ the motion."

main motion

C 36.   The reason for requiring a second to a main motion is to show that someone other than the maker of the motion wishes to consider the ___.

second

C 37.   Mr. Smith has made a main motion to paint the clubroom red. If Ms. Jones wishes to consider this motion, she may ___ the motion by saying "___ ___ ___ ___."

motion

C 38.   There is no need to address the chair and be recognized in order to second a main motion. Immediately after a main motion is made, a member may ___ the motion if he wishes to have it considered.

second · I second the motion

C 39.   It is not necessary to gain recognition to ___ a main motion.

second

C 40.   After the main motion has been seconded, the chair will open the floor for *debate* on the motion. During this period of ___ the members may argue for and against the motion.

second

C 41.   If Ms. Jones makes a motion that you do NOT approve of, then during the ___ period you may gain the floor and argue against it.

debate

C 42. If, instead, you *approve* of a motion that has been made and would like to see it passed, then during the debate period you may argue ＿＿ the motion.

debate

C 43. Besides being used for argument for and against the main motion, the debate period can also be used for *amending* the motion. A formal change or modification of a main motion is called an ＿＿. (Amending will be discussed in Set D.)

for

C 44. The motion before the group at any one moment is sometimes called the *question*. After the debating and amending period is over, the chair will ask the group if they are ready to vote on the ＿＿.

amendment

C 45. When the debate and the amending seem to be over, then the chair will ask the group if they are ready to ＿＿ on the ＿＿.

question or motion

C 46. If the group is ready to vote, they will join in a general chorus of "Question." Upon receiving this approval, the chair will state the question (or motion) again before the vote is taken. The chair will say, "The ＿＿ is. . . ."

vote · question or motion

C 47. After the debate on a main motion has stopped, then the procedure is as follows:
1. The chair will ask if the group is ready ＿＿ ＿＿.
2. The group will answer with "＿＿."
3. The chair will restate the ＿＿ before the vote is taken.

question or motion

C 48. There are two other commonly used ways to close or end debate. A member may move the previous question (which will be discussed in Set E), or a member may simply call

1) to vote (or, for the question) 2) Question 3) question or motion

the question. Debate on a question may be
ended by:
1. the chairman stating, "Are you ready to
vote?"
2. a member moving the previous question
3. a member _____ the question

C 49.   We have discussed the way a chairman   *calling*
may put the question to close debate. To
move the previous question will be discussed
later. Now we will discuss the method of clos-
ing debate by calling the _____.

C 50.   To call the question, a member simply   *question*
states, "I call the question." This means that
he wishes to vote now on the _____ before the
group.

C 51.   After a call for the question, the chair   *question or motion*
will state that the question has been called. If
his statement is followed by a general chorus
of "Question" or "Yes" or by silence, then he
assumes that the group is ready to _____ on
the question.

C 52.   If some of the members wish to con-   *vote*
tinue debate after the question has been
called, they may do so, since "calling the
question" is not a formal motion. If this hap-
pens, then debate will continue until the question is called again, a member moves the previous question, or the chairman puts the question by asking, "Are you ready to _____?"

C 53.   There are, of course, two votes that   *vote*
must be taken: the vote for the motion, or the
affirmative vote, and the vote _____ the motion, or the *negative* vote.

C 54.   The vote may be taken any way the   *against*
the chair sees fit (show of hands, voice vote,

ballot, etc.), but the chair must be sure to call
for both sides of the vote. In other words, he
must call for both the _____ vote and the
negative vote.

C 55.   The reason the chair must always take   *affirmative*
both votes is to give each member a chance to
participate and to signify his approval or dis-
approval of the motion. Even though the
affirmative vote gives the passing majority
needed, it is the chair's duty to call for the
_____ vote.

C 56.   In taking the vote, the affirmative vote   *negative*
must be called for first. After the affirmative
is taken, then the chair will call for the _____
vote.

C 57.   The affirmative vote is taken to deter-   *negative*
mine the number of people _____ the motion,
and the negative vote is taken to determine
the number _____ the motion.

C 58.   The _____ vote is always taken first.   *for · against*

C 59.   When taking a vote, the chairman   *affirmative*
should specify the precise method of voting.
Thus, when taking a vote, the chairman will
say, "All in favor say 'yes,' " or "will stand,"
and then pause to allow time for the members
who are for the motion to _____.

C 60.   After the affirmative vote has been   *vote*
taken, the chairman will say, "All opposed
say 'no.' " This will give the members who are
_____ the motion an opportunity to vote.

C 61.   When taking the vote in a meeting, the   *against*
chair will first call for those in favor of the

motion and then call for those _____ to the motion.

C 62. The two votes called for by the chairman are the affirmative and negative. He calls
for the affirmative vote by saying. "_____
_____ _____ say 'yes.' " He calls for the negative vote by saying, "_____ _____ say 'no.' "

opposed

C 63. A voice vote should NOT be taken in
determining a fraction vote. That is, in trying
to determine if two-thirds or three-fourths of
the members voting are in favor of the motion, the chairman should have the members
either raise their hands or stand rather than
have them _____ "yes" or "no."

*All in favor · All
opposed*

C 64. The vote required to pass a main motion is a simple majority, which is at least one
more than one-half of the members voting. If
the final tally in a vote is 6 affirmative and 5
negative, then the motion is passed by a _____
_____ .

say

C 65. At least one more than one-half of the
members voting for one side is what we call a
_____ _____.

simple majority

C 66. If the following votes would pass by a
simple majority, write "yes"; if they would
not, write "no."
1. 10 affirmative, 8 negative
2. 5 affirmative, 4 negative
3. 8 affirmative, 9 negative

simple majority

C 67. The other vote commonly used in
business meetings is *two-thirds*. If a motion is
passed by two-thirds, it simply means that
two-thirds of the members voted *for* the motion. If the final tally in a vote is 15 affirma-

1) yes 2) yes 3) no

tive and 7 negative, then the vote is passed by
_____ .

C 68.   A simple method for determining a   *two-thirds*
two-thirds vote is to multiply the negative
vote by two. If the product is equal to or less
than the affirmative vote, then the motion is
passed by _____ .

C 69.   If the negative vote is multiplied by   *two-thirds*
two and the product is larger than the affirma-
tive vote, then the motion fails to pass by
_____ .

C 70.   You can easily determine whether a   *two-thirds*
vote passed by two-thirds by multiplying the
negative vote by _____ .

C 71.   If, after multiplying by two, the prod-   *two*
uct is equal to or less than the _____ vote, then
the motion is passed by _____ .

C 72.   There are fifteen members in an orga-   *affirmative · two-*
nization, and they all vote affirmatively or   *thirds*
negatively on a motion. If the motion passes
by *two-thirds*, the affirmative vote has to be
at least _____ votes, and the negative vote
could not be more than _____ votes.

C 73.   If the following votes would pass by   *ten · five*
two-thirds, write "yes"; if not, write "no."
(Remember, multiply the negative vote by
two, and if the product is equal to or less than
the affirmative vote, there is a two-thirds
passing vote.)
1. 10 affirmative, 8 negative
2. 21 affirmative, 7 negative
3. 14 affirmative, 7 negative

C 74.   After the votes have been counted, the chair will announce the results as passed or failed. If the vote required was a simple majority and the final tally was 27 affirmative and 13 negative, then the chair would announce that the motion _____ .

1) no 2) yes 3) yes

C 75.   The chairman must always take both sides of the vote. This means he must take both the affirmative and _____ votes.

passed

C 76.   The term *disposed of* refers to the conclusion of the activities which began when a member addressed the chair for the purpose of proposing some action and which ended when the results of the vote were announced. After the vote has been taken and the results announced, the motion is officially _____ _____ .

negative

C 77.   The only way a person can change his vote is by using a special motion which will be studied later. Therefore, after the chair announces the voting results no one can _____ his vote.

disposed of

C 78.   If the affirmative vote is the only vote that has been taken, a member who voted affirmatively may withdraw his vote before the chairman calls for the _____ vote.

change

C 79.   A member can change his _____ from affirmative to negative, or vice versa, after both votes have been taken and prior to the chairman's announcement of the results.

negative

C 80.   If both votes have been taken, can a member change his vote? Yes or no?

vote

C 81.   If the affirmative vote has been taken,

yes

a member who voted affirmatively can withdraw his _____ and then vote negatively when
the chair asks for the negative vote.

C 82   When can a member change his vote?
(In your own words.)

vote

C 83.   At what point is it out of order for a
member to change his vote? (In your own
words.)

anytime before
the results are
announced

C 84.   Complete the following statements.
1. A statement of a proposed action is a
_____ .
2. Before having the floor, a member must
_____ the chair and be _____ .
3. Immediately after a main motion is made,
a _____ is required.
4. The time during which the members may
argue for and against a motion is the period
of _____ .
5. The two votes which must be taken on a
motion are the _____ _____ and the _____ _____ .

after both votes
have been taken and
the chair has an-
nounced the results

You are now ready to begin Set D, Amending
a Motion.

1) motion, main
motion, or original
main motion 2)
address · recognized
3) second 4) debate
5) affirmative vote
(or vote for the
motion) · negative
vote (or vote against
the motion)

set D

AMENDING A MOTION[1]

Place a card or piece of paper (approximately 3″ x 5″) over the page. Move the card down the page to expose one frame at a time. Read the frame carefully. The blanks in the frame indicate where essential information is missing; the number of blanks indicates the number of words in the desired response. Do not write in the blanks; write your response in the space to the right of the frame. Then move the card down to expose the next frame; as you do so you will also expose the correct answer to the previous frame, which is given in the right-hand column opposite the next frame. Check your answer before continuing the program.

D 1.   An amendment is a proposal for a change or modification of a motion. You may _____ by *adding* something to the motion, *deleting* or *striking* something from the motion, or *substituting* a word, phrase, sentence, paragraph, or section.

D 2.   An amendment is used to change or modify a _____ _____ .

amend

D 3.   If a member wishes to change or modify another member's main motion, he can do so by _____ the motion.

main motion

[1] For a more detailed discussion of this subject, see *Robert's Rules of Order Newly Revised*, **pages** 108-140.

D 4.   To amend a main motion, a member would say, "I move that we amend the motion by . . . ," stating the change he wishes to make in the motion. If he wishes to amend a main motion by striking the word "red," he would say, "I move that we _____ the motion by _____ the word 'red.' "

amending

D 5.   An amendment is a proposal for a _____ or modification of a motion.

amend · striking or deleting

D 6.   An amendment is treated in the same manner as a main motion. Someone other than the maker of the amendment must wish to consider the change; therefore, an amendment requires a _____ .

change

D 7.   The amendment, like the main motion, must be thrown open for _____ after being seconded.

second

D 8.   The amendment and the main motion are similar in that both are introduced by the three words "_____ _____ _____ ," both require a _____ , and both are thrown open for _____ by the group.

debate

D 9.   A formal proposal for action in a business meeting is known as a _____ _____ , and a formal proposal for a change or modification of a motion is called an _____ .

I move that · second · debate

D 10.   We may amend by three methods:
1. *deletion:* taking something from the motion
2. *substitution:* replacing a word, phrase, sentence, etc., of the motion
3. _____ : attaching something new to the motion

main motion · amendment

D 11.   Amendments are used to mold the motion into an acceptable form which will express the will of the organization. We may amend by addition, ____, and ____ .

addition

D 12.   List the *three* methods of amending.

*substitution ·
deletion*

D 13.   Amendments are used to ____ the motion into a form acceptable to at least a majority of the members of the organization.

1) addition 2) substitution 3) deletion

D 14.   The following is an example of an amendment by ____ : "I move that we leave out the word 'farm' in 'farm policy.' "

mold

D 15.   The following is an example of an amendment by ____ ; "I move that we insert the word 'farm' before the word 'policy.' "

deletion

D 16.   If it is necessary to make numerous changes in a main motion, it may be better to substitute a whole new motion rather than make numerous ____ .

addition

D 17.   To change six or eight different words or items in a single motion, it may be best to amend by ____ a whole new motion for the original motion.

amendments

D 18.   Great care should be exercised in amending by substituting a whole new motion for the original motion. To ____ the motion of painting the classroom for the motion of buying a new bus would not be a proper use of this type of amending procedure.

substituting

D 19.   This is an example of an amendment by ____: "I move that we exchange the following motion for the present motion. . . ."

substitute

D 20.   The three methods of amending are (in any order) by ____, by ____, and by ____.

substitution

D 21.   The purpose of amending is to change or modify the main motion so that it is more ____ to a majority of the members of the organization.

substitution · addition · deletion

D 22.   Any amendment that is made must have a second and must be opened for ____ by the group.

acceptable

D 23.   The amendments we have discussed are amendments to the motion itself, or what we call *first degree* amendments. If we wish, however, we may amend a first degree amendment with what we call a *second degree* amendment. There are, therefore, two kinds of amendments: the ____ degree and the ____ degree.

debate

D 24.   Amendments to the motion are called first degree amendments. Amendments to the first degree amendments are called ____ ____ amendments. There can be no third, fourth, fifth, etc., degree amendments.

first · second

D 25.   The amendments applied to the ____ ____ are called first degree amendments and may be amended by ____ ____ amendments.

second degree

D 26.   The amendment in number 1 below is an example of a ____ degree amendment, and number 2 is an example of a ____ degree amendment.
1. "I move that we amend the motion by adding the words 'state farm policy.'"
2. "I move that we amend the amendment by deleting the word 'state.'"

main motion
second degree

D 27.   There can be an amendment to the motion and an amendment to the _____.

first · second

D 28.   There can be a first degree amendment and a second degree amendment but never a _____ degree amendment.

amendment

D 29.   The first degree amendment can be amended, but the _____ degree amendment cannot be amended.

third

D 30.   When the second degree amendment has been disposed of (voted on), then *another* second degree amendment can be made. But remember that the second degree amendment cannot be _____.

second

D 31.   If it is necessary to make a large number of first and second degree amendments, it may be more advantageous to amend by substituting a whole new *motion* for the intended amended _____ _____.

amended

D 32.   When a first degree amendment has been disposed of (voted on), then another _____ _____ amendment can be made.

main motion

D 33.   The main motion, therefore, is amended by the _____ degree amendment. This amendment may then be amended by a _____ degree amendment. But this is as far as we may go, for there can be no _____ degree amendments.

first degree

D 34.   There is really nothing complicated about amending a motion if we remember the following:
1. Amending takes place after the motion has been seconded and the floor is open for _____.
2. A motion may be amended by a _____ degree amendment.

first · second · third

3. After seconding and discussion of the first degree amendment, it may be amended by a _____ degree amendment.

D 35. Amendments must be voted on in *reverse* order. The second degree amendment (if one has been made) must be disposed of first; then after seconding and discussion of the first degree amendment the vote can be taken on the _____ _____ amendment.

debate · first · second

D 36. After taking the vote on the first degree amendment, and, after discussion of the main motion, the vote can then be taken on the _____ _____.

first degree

D 37. If you have made a main motion and I have amended it, which will be voted on first—the main motion or the amendment?

main motion

D 38. If you make a motion and I amend it and then John Doe amends my amendment, in what order will the votes be taken?

the amendment

D 39. In disposing of a motion and its amendments, the _____ _____ _____ is voted on first, then the _____ _____ _____, and finally the motion itself.

1) John Doe's second degree amendment 2) my first degree amendment 3) your motion

D 40. Voting in _____ order is the rule to remember in voting on amendments.

second degree amendment · first degree amendment

D 41. An amendment is made, seconded, and thrown open for debate. This debate must be limited to the debate of the _____ and not extend to a debate of the original motion.

reverse

D 42. The vote required to pass a motion or amendment is a simple majority. If the vote

amendment

on a second degree amendment is 8 affirmative and 7 negative, the amendment _____ by
a simple majority.

D 43.   The vote required to pass a motion is
a _____ _____.

passes

D 44.   The vote required to pass an amendment is a _____ _____.

simple majority

D 45.   A final important rule to remember
about amendments is that all amendments
must be *germane;* that is, an amendment must
be on or relate to the subject to be amended.
All amendments to a motion must be _____ to
the subject of the motion.

simple majority

D 46.   An amendment must be *germane* to
the subject to be amended. A first degree
amendment to a main motion must be _____
to the subject of that main motion.

germane

D 47.   If all _____ _____ amendments must be
germane to the subject of the motion being
amended and all second degree amendments
must be germane to the subject of the first
degree amendments, then all _____ _____
amendments must be germane to the subject
of the motion being amended.

germane

D 48.   All first degree amendments must be
germane to the subject of the main motion,
and all _____ degree amendments must be
germane to the first degree amendment and
also to the main motion.

*first degree · second
degree*

D 49.   If the motion before the group is
whether to buy a new school bus for the
school and someone moves to substitute "a
new water cooler" for "school bus," the

second

amendment would be improper because it is
not germane or related to the _____ of buying
a new school bus for the school.

D 50.   It is possible to make an amendment   *subject*
_____ or relate to the subject being amended
even though this amendment may be hostile
toward or against the wishes of the supporters
of the subject being amended.

D 51.   Amendments may be _____ toward or   *germane*
against the wishes of the supporters of the
subject being amended.

D 52.   On the basis of what you have learned   *hostile*
about amending, complete the following state-
ments:
1. We may amend by: _____, deletion, and
_____.
2. A motion is amended by a _____ _____
amendment.
3. The vote required to pass a motion or an
amendment is a _____ _____.
4. Amendments must be _____ (related) to
the subject being amended.

You are now ready to begin Set E, Classifica-   *1) addition · substi-*
tion of Motions and Privileged Motions.   *tution 2) first*
                                                        degree 3) simple
                                                        majority 4) germane

set E

CLASSIFICATION OF MOTIONS AND PRIVILEGED MOTIONS

Place a card or piece of paper (approximately 3″ x 5″) over the page. Move the card down the page to expose one frame at a time. Read the frame carefully. The blanks in the frame indicate where essential information is missing; the number of blanks indicates the number of words in the desired response. Do not write in the blanks; write your response in the space to the right of the frame. Then move the card down to expose the next frame; as you do so you will also expose the correct answer to the previous frame, which is given in the right-hand column opposite the next frame. Check your answer before continuing the program.

This set will deal generally with the classification, usage, and precedence of motions. Specific rules regarding the vote required, seconding, amendability, debatability, and renewability in the disposition of individual motions are not programmed. This information is available in the Reference Chart for the Most Commonly Used Motions which is available for easy reference on the inside back cover of this text, or in *Robert's Rules or Order Newly Revised,* tinted section following page 292.

I. *Precedence of Motions*[1]

E 1.   For convenience, motions are divided into four classifications: (1) privileged motions, (2) subsidiary motions, (3) incidental motions, and (4) main _____.

---

[1] For a more detailed discussion of this subject, see *Robert's Rules of Order Newly Revised,* pages 48-52.

E 2.   There are how many different classifications of motions? _____

motions

E 3.   The general classifications of motions
are:
1. privileged motions
2. _____ _____
3. incidental motions
4. _____ _____

four

E 4.   List the four general classifications of
motions.
1. _____ _____
2. _____ _____
3. _____ _____
4. _____ _____

2) subsidiary mo-
tions 4) main
motions

E 5.   In discussing classification of motions,
the terms "in order" and "out of order" will
be used. "In order" is one of the terms used
in discussing _____ of motions.

1) privileged mo-
tions 2) subsidiary
motions 3) inciden-
tal motions 4) main
motions

E 6.   If a group is following the proper
order of business in a meeting, then the action
of the group would be "in _____."

classification

E 7.   A member who moves a motion which
should not be considered at that time should
be ruled "out of _____."

order

E 8.   "In order" and "out of order" are two
terms used in parliamentary procedure. Explain, in your own words, what each term
means.

order

E 9.   Each general classification of motions —privileged, subsidiary, incidental, and main— has a general status or relevance of disposition to other motions. The term *precedence* as used in parliamentary practice deals with this status. Main motions do not take precedence over any of the other three classes of motions. A main motion, therefore, would not take _____ over a privileged motion.

"In order" means the motion or procedure is proper and should be used. "Out of order" means the motion or procedure is improper and should not be used.

E 10.   If a motion fulfills all the qualifications of procedure including precedence, then we generally say that the motion is _____ _____.

precedence

E 11.   For the moment, let us consider only the correct order of precedence of the four general classifications of motions. A privileged motion ranks highest in the order of _____.

in order

E 12.   A privileged motion does not relate to the question pending before a group but is of such great importance to the group that it takes _____ over all subsidiary and main motions.

precedence

E 13.   Subsidiary motions do apply to main motions. Since subsidiary motions apply to main motions, they supersede main motions in the order of _____.

precedence

E 14.   Subsidiary motions may modify main motions, or postpone action on them, or refer them to committees for investigation and a report, etc. Therefore, _____ motions apply to main motions.

precedence

E 15.   Must a subsidiary motion (assuming it is in order) be *disposed of* before or after the disposition of the main motion to which it applies?

subsidiary

E 16.   Privileged motions take precedence
over all other motions. Subsidiary motions
must be disposed of before the main motions
to which they apply can be disposed of.
Therefore, privileged motions take precedence
over subsidiary and main _____, and subsidiary
motions take _____ over main motions.

before

E 17.   The fourth general classification of
motions is the incidental motion. This motion
arises out of another motion pending before
the group and cannot be assigned a position
of _____ over other motions.

*motions · prece-
dence*

E 18.   An example of an incidental motion
may be helpful at this point. When a person
who has not been recognized by the *chairman*
begins to speak, another member may rise to
a "point of order." This action is an example
of an incidental motion and would make the
first member follow proper order in gaining
recognition of the _____.

precedence

E 19.   Incidental motions can take precedence over all motions to which they are legitimately incidental but can yield precedence to
_____ motions.

chairman

E 20.   Incidental motions can arise out of or
be a result of almost any main, subsidiary, or
privileged motions. However, with the exception of a "division of the assembly" motion,
privileged motions take _____ over incidental
motions. (See *Robert's Rules of Order Newly
Revised*, pages 62-64.)

privileged

E 21.   Look at the four classifications of
motions this way. The classification that ranks
highest in precedence is the *privileged motions*. Next in rank are *two* classifications:
incidental motions, when they arise out of
pending motions, and *subsidiary motions*,

precedence

when no incidental motions are pending.
Finally, when none of the other three kinds
of motions is pending, there are the _____
motions.

E 22.   Now, as a brief review of the four   *main*
classifications of motions, the privileged mo-
tions take precedence over _____, subsidiary,
and incidental motions.

E 23.   Main motions do not take _____ over   *main*
any of the other three classifications of
motions.

E 24.   Subsidiary motions take precedence   *precedence*
over _____ motions but yield precedence to
privileged motions.

E 25.   Subsidiary motions are subsidiary to   *main*
(or in some way can affect) original _____
motions.

E 26.   Incidental motions can be incidental   *main*
to privileged _____ and _____ motions and
should be disposed of as they arise.

E 27.   NOTE: Not all subsidiary motions   *motions · main*
are subject to other subsidiary motions of
higher precedence; that is, not all subsidiary
motions can have other _____ motions applied
to them. For example, you can not postpone
to a certain time the motion to postpone indefinitely.

II. *Privileged Motions*[1]

---

[1] For a more detailed discussion of this subject, see
Robert's Rules of Order Newly Revised, pages 56-58.

E 28. There are five often used privileged
motions in parliamentary _____.

subsidiary

E 29. Now, let's investigate the various motions that are classified as privileged motions.
Remember, these motions are privileged because they are of great importance to the
group and thus rank highest in the order of
_____.

procedure

E 30. The privileged motions are, in order
of precedence among themselves: (1) motion
to fix the time to which to adjourn, (2) motion to adjourn, (3) motion to recess, (4)
question of privilege, and (5) orders of the
day. REMEMBER: these five motions are
listed in the _____ of precedence among themselves.

precedence

E 31. The motion to fix the time to which
to adjourn ranks highest in the order of _____
among privileged motions. (See *Robert's
Rules of Order Newly Revised*, page 207.)

order

E 32. To fix the time to which _____ _____ is
the only motion that is in order after a motion to adjourn or end the meeting has been
made, seconded, and voted on, but before the
chair has declared the meeting adjourned.

precedence

E 33. To fix _____ _____ _____ _____ _____
_____ is not an amendment to the motion to
adjourn.

to adjourn

E 34. To _____ _____ _____ _____ _____ _____
_____ is the same as moving the time the group
will meet again.

*the time to which to
adjourn*

E 35. It is important to fix the time to
which to adjourn if the organization does not

*fix the time to
which to adjourn*

meet at a regular time or date. An organization that does not have regularly scheduled
meetings would have to vote at each meeting
on the _____ and date of its next meeting.

E 36.   If we want to hold our next meeting
at 7:00 p.m. on April 1, the motion to fix
____ ____ ____ ____ ____ ____ would be,
"I move that when we adjourn, we stand ad-
journed until 7:00 p.m. on April 1."

time

E 37.   How would you move to fix the time
to which to adjourn for 1:00 p.m. on October
5 in the auditorium? Write out your motion.

*the time to which to
adjourn*

E 38. The privileged motion that takes precedence over ALL other motions is the mo-
tion to ____ ____ ____ ____ ____ ____
____.

*"I move that when
we adjourn we stand
adjourned until 1:00
p.m. on October 5
in the auditorium."*

E 39.   To fix the time to which to adjourn
is the only motion that can be made after the
motion to adjourn is passed. Therefore, to
____ ____ ____ ____ ____ ____ ____ takes
precedence over all other privileged, subsid-
iary, and main motions.

*fix the time to
which to adjourn*

E 40.   To fix the time to which to adjourn
takes ____ over all other privileged motions.

*fix the time to
which to adjourn*

E 41.   The second motion to be considered
under privileged motions is the motion to
adjourn. To ____ means to end a meeting
permanently.

precedence

E 42.   During the course of a meeting, we
come to a point when we wish to end the
meeting. The motion to adjourn is then used
to ____ a meeting.

adjourn

E 43. The main purpose of the motion to adjourn is to *end* a meeting; however, it may also be used to ＿＿＿ discussion on a subject.

end

E 44. The motion to adjourn can be made at any time during the meeting. Thus, if the members want to go home, one member would simply stand and move, "I move that we ＿＿＿." (This motion naturally needs a second and a vote. See *Robert's Rules of Order Newly Revised*, page 199.)

end or stop

E 45. Some clubs do not meet at a regular time or date; therefore, the members would have to fix the time to which to adjourn before they ＿＿＿ or end the meeting.

adjourn

E 46. In determining precedence, the motion to adjourn would be ranked second. The first ranking motion is to fix ＿＿＿ ＿＿＿ ＿＿＿ ＿＿＿ ＿＿＿ ＿＿＿.

adjourn

E 47. If you will remember, the motion to adjourn was stated as being in order anytime during the meeting. This is because the motion to adjourn takes ＿＿＿ over all main, subsidiary, incidental, and privileged motions except the privileged motion to fix the time to which to adjourn.

the time to which to adjourn

E 48. Let's try the first two privileged motions again. To fix the time to which to adjourn takes precedence over all other motions; therefore, would the motion to fix the time to which to adjourn take precedence over the motion to adjourn? Yes or no?

precedence

E 49. The motion to adjourn takes precedence over all other motions except the motion to ＿＿＿ ＿＿＿ ＿＿＿ ＿＿＿ ＿＿＿ ＿＿＿ ＿＿＿.

yes

E 50.   Now, decide the following case on the basis of the precedence of motions. In a meeting, one member is discussing a main motion when another member moves to adjourn. Assuming the speaker discussing the main motion was not interrupted, is the motion to adjourn in order?

fix the time to which to adjourn

E 51.   To end a meeting permanently, we would use the motion to _____ .

yes

E 52.   If we do not want to adjourn permanently but would like to take a break, we can *dismiss* temporarily through a motion to recess. To recess means that the meeting is temporarily _____ and will reassemble at a later time. (See *Robert's Rules of Order Newly Revised*, page 196.)

adjourn

E 53.   It should be remembered that the motion to _____ only temporarily dismisses a group.

dismissed or adjourned

E 54.   To recess means we are temporarily *dismissed* for a certain time and will reconvene. It does NOT mean we are permanently _____ as we would be if we adjourned.

recess

E 55.   To temporarily end a meeting for a period of time, we would use the motion to _____ .

dismissed

E 56.   When you move to recess, you should state the length of the recess. It can be for a few minutes or several hours, but recess means the group is temporarily _____ and will reassemble.

recess

E 57.   A temporary disbanding of the meet-

dismissed

ing can be brought about by using the motion to _____.

E 58. If it were hot and you had been in a meeting for a couple of hours and faced the possibility of another two hours in the meeting, you could temporarily end the meeting by moving to _____ for fifteen minutes.

recess

E 59. To make the motion to recess for five minutes, you would say, "I move that we recess _____ _____ _____."

recess

E 60. Write out a motion to recess two hours for dinner.

for five minutes

E 61. To recess is the third ranking privileged motion in the order of _____. Thus, a motion to recess yields precedence to the motion to fix the time to which to adjourn and the motion to adjourn.

"I move that we recess two hours for dinner."

E 62. What do we mean when we say that the motion to adjourn takes precedence over the motion to recess? (In your own words.)

precedence

E 63. Which motion takes precedence—fix the time to which to adjourn or recess?

If both motions are made, the motion to adjourn is considered first.

E 64. The fourth highest ranking motion in the order of precedence is the *question of privilege*. Such a motion would, for example, allow you to open the window if it is too hot. The _____ _____ _____, then, is the fourth highest ranking motion.

fix the time to which to adjourn

E 65. The question of privilege enables the

question of privilege

chairman to dispose of a certain request made
by a ＿＿＿ of the organization.

E 66.   If the room is too hot, a member may
rise and ask the chairman if he may raise a
window. This would be a question of ＿＿＿.

member

E 67.   If there is no objection by another
member, the chairman may grant the motion
to raise the window, which would be a ＿＿＿
＿＿＿ privilege.

privilege

E 68.   In making the motion to raise the window, you would say, "I rise to a question
＿＿＿ ＿＿＿." After the chair asks you to state
your question, you would proceed to say it
was too hot and ask for the window to be
raised.

question of

E 69.   If a member objects to having the window raised, the chair may ask for a second and
have the members vote on whether to grant
the question ＿＿＿ ＿＿＿ to raise the window.
(See *Robert's Rules of Order Newly Revised*,
page 191.)

of privilege

E 70.   If the members grant the ＿＿＿ of privilege, the window is raised; if they do not
grant the ＿＿＿ of ＿＿＿, the window is not
raised.

of privilege

E 71.   How would you use the question of
privilege to change seats because it is too cold
where you are sitting? Write out your motion.

*question · question ·
privilege*

E 72.   A question of privilege relates to the
group's or the individual's comfort. It may
also relate to charges against an individual's
character which, if true, might incapacitate
him for membership. If someone in your

*"I rise to a question
of privilege. May I
change seats due to
the cold air in this
part of the room?"*

organization called you a traitor, you could
use the privileged motion of ____ ____ ____
to defend yourself.

E 73.   Now, let's review the precedence of
privileged motions. If a member moves to
recess and after this a member rises for a question of privilege, the chairman would rule the
____ ____ ____ out of order because a motion to recess takes ____ over a question of
privilege.

question of privilege

E 74.   Does the motion to adjourn or a question of privilege take precedence?

question of privilege
· precedence

E 75.   If you wish to end the present meeting and meet again at the next regularly scheduled time, you would use the motion to ____.

adjourn

E 76.   If you wish to end the meeting but
your organization does not have a regularly
scheduled time or place to meet, you could
move to adjourn and then move to ____ ____
____ ____ ____ to adjourn.

adjourn

E 77.   Can you move to fix the time to
which to adjourn after a motion to adjourn
has been made? Yes or no?

fix the time to
which

E 78.   Can you move to adjourn during old
business and still be in order? Yes or no?

yes

E 79.   Rank the following privileged motions
from highest to lowest (1 to 4) in the order
of precedence: question of privilege, adjourn,
fix the time to which to adjourn, recess.

yes

E 80.   Now list the *first four* privileged motions in accordance with their ranking to each
other and to all other motions.

*1) fix the time to
which to adjourn
2) adjourn 3) recess
4) question of
privilege*

E 81.   The fifth and final privileged motion
is *orders of the day*. This motion is the lowest
ranking privileged ____.

*1) fix the time to
which to adjourn
2) adjourn 3) recess
4) question of privi-
lege*

E 82.   A call for the orders of the day is a
demand for the organization to conform to its
program or order of *business*. It is made when
the organization is varying from the order of
____.

motion

E 83.   If an organization does not have an
order of business or the order ____ ____ is
not being varied, then this motion could not
be made.

business

E 84.   This motion, orders of the day, is
rather exceptional in that a single member has
the right to demand that the group conform
to the order of business. A call for the orders
____ ____ ____ takes precedence over all
other motions except adjourn, recess, question of privilege, and ____ ____ ____ ____
____ ____ ____.

of business

E 85.   It is the duty of the chairman to announce the business to come before the
group. If he does this, there will be very little
occasion ever to call for the ____ ____ ____
____.

*of the day · fix the
time to which to
adjourn*

E 86.   If a special time has been assigned to
debate a particular question and the chairman
fails to notice that it is time to take up the
motion or thinks the members are too inter-

orders of the day

ested in the pending question to be interrupted, any member has a right to call for the
____ ____ ____ ____.

E 87.   If the orders of the day are called, then
the group will stop debate on the pending
question and proceed with the ____ of business. (See *Robert's Rules of Order Newly
Revised*, page 186.)

orders of the day

E 88.   If the call for the orders of the day is
called but then set aside by a two-thirds vote,
the group will continue with the pending business. A second call for the orders of the day is
not allowed until the pending ____ is disposed of. (The privileged motion of orders of
the day can be treated in several ways and has
various exceptions to its disposition; further
information about this motion can be found
in *Robert's Rules of Order Newly Revised*,
pages 186-191.)

order

E 89.   We have now discussed all five of the
privileged motions. They are, in their order of
precedence:
1. fix the time to which to adjourn
2. ____
3. ____
4. question of privilege
5. ____ ____ the day.

business

E 90.   Review the material in this set by
completing the following statements:
1. The four general classifications of motions:
are: ____ ____, subsidiary motions, ____
____ and ____ ____.
2. ____ ____ ____ refers to a motion or procedure which is improper and should not be
used.
3. ____ ____ take precedence over all other
motions.
4. Rank order the following privileged mo-

*2) adjourn 3) recess
5) orders of*

tions from highest to lowest in the order of precedence: question of privilege, adjourn, orders of the day, fix the time to which to adjourn, recess.

You are now ready to begin Set F, Subsidiary Motions.

1) privileged motions · incidental motions · main motions 2) out of order 3) privileged motions 4) fix the time to which to adjourn, adjourn, recess, question of privilege, orders of the day

set F

SUBSIDIARY MOTIONS[1]

Place a card or piece of paper (approximately 3″ x 5″) over the page. Move the
card down the page to expose one frame at a time. Read the frame carefully.
The blanks in the frame indicate where essential information is missing; the
number of blanks indicates the number of words in the desired response. Do
not write in the blanks; write your response in the space to the right of the
frame. Then move the card down to expose the next frame; as you do so you
will also expose the correct answer to the previous frame, which is given in the
right-hand column opposite the next frame. Check your answer before continuing the program.

F 1.   Privileged motions were the first motions we examined. The second general classification of motions to be considered is that of
the subsidiary motions. These motions alter
or in some way affect main _____.

F 2.   Subsidiary motions can be applied to   *motions*
any main motion; since they supersede or
take _____ over the main motion, they must
be disposed of before the main motion can
be acted upon.

F 3.   If a main motion is on the floor being   *precedence*
debated and someone makes the following
motion: "I move that we lay this motion on

[1] For a more detailed discussion of this subject, see
Robert's Rules of Order Newly Revised, pages 52–56.

the table,'' would this subsidiary motion if
carried affect the main motion? Yes or no?

F 4.　To move that a main motion be laid   *yes*
on the table does, of course, affect the main
motion. The first subsidiary motion, in an
order of precedence among themselves, is the
motion to lay on the ＿＿＿.

F 5.　′Before we can take a motion from the   *table*
table (to be discussed later), it must be ＿＿＿
on the table. (See *Robert's Rules of Order
Newly Revised*, pages 177-185.)

F 6.　When we want to lay aside a motion   *laid*
in order to consider more urgent business, we
can move to lay the motion on the ＿＿＿.

F 7.　The motion lay on the table can be   *table*
applied to any ＿＿＿ motion.

F 8.　To lay a motion on the table, you   *main*
would say, "I move that we ＿＿＿ ＿＿＿ ＿＿＿
＿＿＿ ＿＿＿ ＿＿＿.''

F 9.　If a member has made a main motion   *lay the motion on
to buy a new book but you think the group   the table*
should vote on increasing dues first, you could
move to lay the main ＿＿＿ ＿＿＿ ＿＿＿ ＿＿＿.

F 10.　After the vote on raising dues has been   *motion on the table*
taken, then you or some other member could
move to take from the table the motion to
buy a new book. The more urgent ＿＿＿ of
raising dues has been disposed of, and now the
group is ready to consider buying a new book.

F 11.　When we lay a motion on the table, it   *business, question,
can be taken from the table anytime during   or motion*

new or unfinished business. In this way the organization can lay *aside* one motion in order to consider a more important or urgent motion and then return to the motion that was laid ____.

F 12. If we lay a motion on the table during the first part of new business, can we take that particular motion from the table during the latter part of new business during the same meeting? Yes or no?	*aside*
F 13. The length of time a motion is laid ____ ____ ____ makes no difference in the status of the motion.	*yes*
F 14. If at the July meeting we voted to lay on the table the motion to buy a new book for the club, could we leave it there until new business in the August meeting? Yes or no?	*on the table*
F 15. NOTE: There are specific time limitations on how long a motion remains laid on the ____. (See *Robert's Rules of Order Newly Revised*, pages 181-182 for these limitations.)	*yes*
F 16. When you wish to lay a motion aside temporarily, or, in other words, *table the motion*, you would say, "I move to ____ ____ ____ . . . ," stating the motion to be laid aside.	*table*
F 17. If a motion has been taken from the table during new business today, it would be out of order to consider a motion to table ____ ____ again until some material progress had been made on the question.	*table the motion*
F 18. To lay on the table is the highest ranking subsidiary motion, yielding only to the	*the motion*

privileged motions, and should be considered
immediately upon its being moved. To _____
_____ _____ _____ takes precedence over all
motions except _____ motions.

F 19.   Since this motion needs only a simple
majority to pass, there is danger that it may
be improperly used to suppress debate on a
question. Extreme caution should be taken to
ensure that the motion to _____ _____ _____
_____ fulfills its objective of laying aside pending business in order to consider more urgent
matters.

*lay on the table ·
privileged*

F 20.   If a main motion has been amended or
is in the act of being amended (an amendment
is under debate) and a motion to lay on the
table is passed, then the main motion and all
the amendments (passed and proposed) are
laid on the _____.

lay on the table

F 21.   If you want to put aside a motion,
you would move to table _____ _____, or lay
on the table.

table

F 22.   Does the motion to lay on the table or
the motion to adjourn take precedence?

the motion

F 23.   If you wish to delay action on a motion only temporarily, you would move to
_____ _____ _____.

adjourn

F 24.   Now, let's move on to the second
ranking subsidiary motion, which is to move
the previous question. This motion ranks
_____ in precedence among subsidiary motions.

table the motion

F 25.   Members may call "Question" to indi-

second

cate to the chairman that they are ready to
_____ on the question.

F 26.   A member can move to vote _____ by   *vote*
saying, "I move the previous question."

F 27.   To make a subsidiary motion to vote   *immediately or now*
immediately on the motion being debated,
you would say, "I move the _____ _____."

F 28.   To move the previous question, if   *previous question*
passed, stops debate on the question and
brings it to an immediate _____.

F 29.   To stop the debate and amending of   *vote*
a motion, you would say, "I move the _____
_____."

F 30.   Moving the previous question means   *previous question*
you wish to vote _____ on the pending motion.

F 31.   If the motion to move the previous   *immediately or now*
_____ fails to pass by a two-thirds vote, then
debate will continue on the original motion
as if the previous question had never been
moved. (See *Robert's Rules of Order Newly
Revised*, pages 167-177.)

F 32.   To move the previous question applies   *question*
only to the question pending before the group
unless otherwise qualified. If a main motion
has been made and an amendment to this
main motion is being debated, a call for the
previous _____, if passed, would mean an immediate vote only on the amendment.

F 33.   Anyone moving the previous question   *question*
would use the form of, "I move (or demand
or call for) the _____ _____ on . . . ," specify-

ing the motion or motions on which it is desired to vote immediately.

F 34.   If the member calling for the previous question does not specify the exact motion, then to what motion is it understood to apply? (Answer in your own words.)

previous question

F 35.   Sometimes a member moves the previous question because he feels that, if the group votes on the pending question immediately, the motion before the group will fail. If the motion to move the previous question is passed, does this mean the group is in favor of the motion on which the previous question is demanded? Yes or no?

the motion pending before the group at the time the previous question is called

F 36.   The subsidiary motion to move the previous question yields to all of the privileged motions but takes precedence over all other subsidiary motions that are amendable or debatable except to lay ____ ____ ____ .

no

F 37.   If the previous question is *ordered* on more than one question, then its effect is not exhausted until all the questions are voted on or disposed of in some other way (i.e., lay on the table). In moving the previous question, a member may ____ an immediate vote on several questions.

on the table

F 38.   There is one limitation of time to the previous question when it is applied to several questions. If the meeting adjourns before all the questions are brought before the group, then the ____ ____ is exhausted. This means that the passage of the previous question is no longer in effect at the next meeting, and any remaining questions are open to debate and amendment.

order or demand

F 39.   If a group was debating a main motion and then passed the motion to move the previous ———— and further passed the motion to lay the motion on the table, the main motion and previous question would be tabled.

previous question

F 40.   If this tabled motion is brought back before the group at the same meeting it must be ———— on immediately because the effect of the previous question is still in force.

question

F 41.   If the tabled motion is brought back from the table at another meeting the effect of the ———— ———— is not in force and the main motion is subject to further debate, amendments, etc. (See *Robert's Rules of Order Newly Revised*, pages 167-177.)

voted

F 42.   Let's briefly review the precedence of motions again. The privileged motions take precedence over the subsidiary motions. The order of precedence of the privileged motions is:
1. fix the ———— ———— ———— ———— ————
2. ———— (permanently end a meeting)
3. ———— (temporarily dismiss a group)
4. question of ————
5. ———— ———— ———— day

previous question

F 43.   The first two subsidiary motions in their order of precedence are:
1. lay on the ————
2. previous ————

1) time to which to adjourn 2) adjourn 3) recess 4) privilege 5) orders of the

F 44.   The third subsidiary motion in the order of precedence is the motion to limit (or extend) debate. The third highest ranking subsidiary motion is to ———— (or extend) ————.

1) table 2) question

F 45.   The motion to limit debate may be used to limit the time for debating the mo-

limit · debate

tion. The time available for debate on any motion could be ＿＿ by saying, "I move that we limit debate to five minutes." (Of course, a second and other requirements must be fulfilled. (See *Robert's Rules of Order Newly Revised*, pages 161-166.)

F 46.   To extend debate we would simply say, "I move that we ＿＿ debate to five minutes."

limited or shortened

F 47.   We can restrict or extend the time for debate on a debatable motion by moving to ＿＿ or ＿＿ debate.

extend

F 48.   This motion to limit or extend debate may also be used to restrict the number of speakers. If you want to limit debate to only five people, you would say, "I move that we ＿＿ ＿＿ to ＿＿ ＿＿." If you wish to extend this limit to ten people, you would say after five people had debated, "I move that we ＿＿ ＿＿ to ＿＿ ＿＿."

limit · extend

F 49.   How would you move to limit debate to three people with each of them having only five minutes to speak? (In your own words.)

limit debate · five people · extend debate · ten people

F 50.   Any motion restricting the time a person can speak, the number of speakers, or the length of speeches in words, etc., would be a subsidiary motion to ＿＿ ＿＿.

"I move that we limit debate to three people with each of them having only five minutes to speak."

F 51.   Even after the adoption of a motion limiting debate, it is in order to make any of the other subsidiary motions on the pending question. If the motion to which limited debate was applied has not been disposed of before the end of the limited time, then at

limit debate

that time the chair should call for an immediate _____ .

F 52.   When the time (speaker, length of
speeches, etc.) limit has expired, no further
amendments or extensions can be made, and
an _____ vote is taken unless someone moves
to reconsider the vote to limit debate or extend debate. (See *Robert's Rules of Order
Newly Revised*, pages 164-165.)

vote

F 53.   To place limits on or extend the limits
of a question can be accomplished by the motion to _____ or _____ _____. This is the third
highest ranking subsidiary motion in the order
of _____ .

immediate

F 54.   If you want to restrict the number of
people who will be allowed to debate a topic,
you would use the subsidiary motion to _____
_____ .

*limit · extend de-
bate · precedence*

F 55.   The motion to postpone definitely (or
to a certain time) is the next highest ranking
_____ motion.

limit debate

F 56.   The motion to postpone _____ is used
to delay action on a main motion until a later
time and/or date.

subsidiary

F 57.   To delay action on a main motion until a later date is done by postponing _____ (to
a certain _____).

definitely

F 58.   A specific date or time is always stated
in the motion to postpone _____ .

definitely · time

F 59.   You must state the specific date or
_____ at which you wish to resume consider-

definitely

ation of a motion when you move to _____
_____.

F 60.   If you wish to debate a main motion
during the last thirty minutes of the meeting,
you would move to _____ the debate of the
motion until the last thirty minutes. (See
Robert's Rules of Order Newly Revised, pages
150-161.)

*time · postpone
definitely*

F 61.   The meeting is to adjourn at 2:00 p.m.
You wish to postpone debate on a main motion until the last ten minutes of the meeting
and would therefore move to _____ debate of
the motion until 1:50 p.m.

postpone

F 62.   In moving to resume consideration of
a main motion at a later time, you would say,
"I move that we _____ the question . . . ,"
stating the date and/or time for reconsider-
ation.

postpone

F 63.   To delay action on a motion until a
certain time, you would use the motion to
_____ _____.

postpone

F 64.   If you wish to postpone the pending
question until after a talk by Dr. Smith, you
would simply say, "_____ _____ _____ _____
_____ the question until after Dr. Smith's
talk."

postpone definitely

F 65.   If you wish to postpone the question
to the next meeting, the form of the motion
would be, "I move that we _____ the question
to the _____ _____." The postponed motion
would then become a general order for that
meeting, taking precedence over new business.

*I move that we post-
pone*

F 66.   When you move to postpone a question _____, giving the next meeting as the time for bringing up the matter, you are in fact stating that the organization make the postponed question part of the next meeting's business.

postpone · next meeting

F 67.   By designating a particular time and date to consider a motion, you are making it an "order of the day." If it is not disposed of then, it becomes old _____ at the next meeting.

definitely

F 68.   If you wish to ensure that a question will not be crowded out by other matters, you would add to the motion to postpone _____ the phrase "and be made a special order."

business

F 69.   A motion to consider a question during the last thirty minutes of a meeting could be, "I move that the question be postponed and be made a _____ _____ of business for the last thirty minutes of this meeting."

definitely

F 70.   To postpone to a certain time does not automatically make the motion a special order. If you wish to make it a _____ order, then you must specify it as such.

special order

F 71.   If a motion is designated as a special _____, the vote required is two-thirds; to postpone definitely requires only a simple majority. (See *Robert's Rules of Order Newly Revised*, page 153.)

special

F 72.   Before going on to the last three subsidiary motions, let's review the privileged and subsidiary motions already covered. Do the privileged motions take precedence over the subsidiary motions? Yes or no?

order

F 73.   List the privileged motions in their order of precedence:
1. ____ ____ ____ ____ ____ ____ ____
2. ____
3. ____
4. question ____ ____
5. orders ____ ____ ____

yes

F 74.   The first four subsidiary motions are:
1. lay ____ ____ ____
2. previous ____
3. ____ (or extend) ____
4. postpone ____

1) fix the time to which to adjourn 2) adjourn 3) recess 4) of privilege 5) of the day

F 75.   Is the motion to adjourn in order at any time after the reading and approval of the minutes? Yes or no?

1) on the table 2) question 3) limit · debate 4) definitely

F 76.   To end the meeting temporarily for a coffee break, you would use the motion to ____.

yes

F 77.   If you want to close debate and vote immediately on a *question*, you would move the ____ ____.

recess

F 78.   If you want to set aside a pending question in order to consider more urgent matters, you would use the motion to ____ ____ ____ ____.

previous question

F 79.   If someone calls you a traitor or makes other derogatory remarks about you, you could rise to a ____ ____ ____ in order to defend yourself.

lay on the table

F 80.   What motion would you use to designate the time the next meeting would be held?

question of privilege

F 81. Does the motion to recess or the motion to limit debate take precedence?

fix the time to which to adjourn

F 82. When a motion is on the floor being debated and another motion is made, one way to determine if the second motion is proper is to consider the _____ of the two motions.

recess

F 83. Now we will continue to investigate the rest of the subsidiary motions in their order of _____. The next motion is to refer (or commit) to a committee. (See *Robert's Rules of Order Newly Revised*, pages 140-150.)

precedence

F 84. One of the reasons for referring a subject to a committee is to have it thoroughly investigated. Thus the motion to refer _____ _____ _____ could be used if the group wants more research done.

precedence

F 85. If we allow a committee to bring in additional information on the subject being debated, this action means that the subject was originally _____ to a _____ for investigation.

to a committee

F 86. If we pass the motion to _____ _____ _____ _____, this action means that the committee should further investigate and study the motion before it is again discussed by the entire group.

referred · committee

F 87. The committee or *group* to which a motion is referred is generally smaller than the whole _____.

refer to a committee

F 88. Another reason for referring a subject to a committee is to save time during the regular meeting and yet fully discover all the various facts about the subject. A smaller group

group or organization

known as a _____ can investigate the subject
and report its findings to the larger group.

F 89.   How many people will be on the com-   *committee*
mittee, when the committee will report, and
any other necessary information can be designated by the person making the motion. He
could, for example, say, "I move that the
motion . . . be referred _____ _____ _____ of
three persons to report at the next meeting."

F 90.   If the person making the motion to   *to a committee*
refer to a committee does not specify how
many persons are to be on the committee or
when the report is due, the chairman assumes
this duty. Therefore, the number, date, etc.,
of the committee can be designated by the
_____.

F 91.   If the committee members are not   *chairman*
designated, the chairman may refer the mo-
tion to an already established committee,
or he may ask for nominations to serve on a
_____ to investigate the subject.

F 92.   A good general rule to follow in desig-   *committee*
nating a leader of a committee is to name the
leader first and then the rest of the committee. This way, the leader will always be the
_____ person named by the chairman.

F 93.   If a person is interested enough in   *first*
having further information on a main motion
that he moves the motion be referred to a
committee, he is indicating a willingness to
serve on the _____.

F 94.   Generally, the maker of the motion to   *committee*
_____ _____ _____ _____ either has knowledge
about the question or an interest in it and
thus would be a good member of the committee.

F 95.   The maker of the motion to _____
_____ _____ _____ may designate the members
to be on the committee (subject to approval
of the group) in order to guarantee that the
committee members are not hostile toward
the question to be investigated.

refer to a committee

F 96.   A hostile committee is one that is
_____ the adoption of the subject under
discussion.

refer to a committee

F 97.   Since a _____ committee is against the
question, it may therefore cause the question
to be lost because of a negative report, no
report, etc.

against

F 98.   On occasion, the entire group or organization may wish to consider a question
informally as a *committee*. When the whole
group wishes to discuss a question informally,
the group moves to a _____ of the whole.

hostile

F 99.   Committee of the whole means that
every member present will be considered a
member of the _____.

committee

F 100.   The motion committee of the whole
and the motion to refer to a _____ are equal
in precedence.

committee

F 101.   A committee of the whole does not
limit the number of members on the _____;
instead, all the members of the group are
members of the committee.

committee

F 102.   Unlike the motion to refer to a committee, the motion committee of the whole
means that all the members of the group will
be members of the committee of the _____
and that the subject will be discussed NOT in

committee

the future but immediately. (Exception: the group may wait until other regular business is finished.)

F 103. The motion committee of the ＿＿＿ is used when an organization wishes to discuss the pending question informally.

whole

F 104. To move into a ＿＿＿ ＿＿＿ ＿＿＿ whole enables the members to discuss a given motion freely and informally without having to record the discussion officially.

whole

F 105. The motion ＿＿＿ of the ＿＿＿ was first used in the late sixteenth and early seventeenth centuries to enable members of the British House of Commons to attack the Crown without running the risk of losing their heads.

committee of the

F 106. Today, in the legislatures of states which require the admission of the press at all regular meetings, the senators may move to a ＿＿＿ ＿＿＿ ＿＿＿ ＿＿＿ in order to discuss state business without the press being present.

committee · whole

F 107. Within an organization where each member can speak only once on a subject (for example, the U.S. Senate), moving to a ＿＿＿ ＿＿＿ ＿＿＿ ＿＿＿ enables a person to speak as often as he wishes.

committee of the whole

F 108. Consensus means that the members agree without *voting*. If a group cannot arrive at a consensus, then the group must ＿＿＿ in order to arrive at a solution (majority rule).

committee of the whole

F 109. The committee of the whole tries to arrive at a consensus, but if it cannot, it must

vote

_____ on the solution and try to get a majority
to favor one single solution.

F 110. The committee of the _____ tries to
arrive at a consensus.

vote

F 111. The committee of the whole does not
make a report as such; rather, the whole
group discusses the pending motion in an in-
formal atmosphere. Good group discussion
rules should apply during the discussion period, and the group should try to solve the
problem by reaching a _____ rather than by
voting.

whole

F 112. While a group is in a *committee* of the
whole, the regular chairman relinquishes his
"chair" to a temporary chairman of the _____.

consensus

F 113. When a _____ _____ _____ _____ wishes
to adjourn, a motion is made that the committee rise and report.

committee

F 114. The motion to rise in a _____ _____
_____ _____ is equivalent to the motion to adjourn in a regular business meeting and is in
order at any time.

*committee of the
whole*

F 115. We have considered two motions to
refer business to a committee. They are: (1)
refer to a _____ and (2) _____ _____ _____
_____.

*committee of the
whole*

F 116. These two motions to refer rank the
_____ in the order of precedence.

*1) committee 2)
committee of the
whole*

F 117. Both of these motions deal with estab-
lishing a _____ to investigate the subject.

same

F 118. In order to obtain further information by having representatives of the group investigate the main motion, we would use the subsidiary motion to ____ ____ ____ ____.

committee

F 119. The two motions that refer main motions to a committee are:
1. ____ ____ ____ committee
2. committee ____ ____ ____

refer to a committee

F 120. The motions to refer yield to all privileged motions and to the following subsidiary motions:
1. lay on the ____
2. previous ____
3. ____ (or extend) debate
4. ____ ____ ____ certain time

1) refer to a 2) of the whole

F 121. If, after a motion to refer ____ ____ ____ has been made, seconded, and stated by the chairman, another member rises and moves to proceed into a committee of the ____, would the motion committee of the whole take precedence? Yes or no? (Remember: both rank equally in precedence.)

1) table 2) question 3) limit 4) postpone to a

F 122. If you wish to have five members investigate a subject and report to the organization at the next meeting, you would rise and say, "I move that we ____ this question to a ____ of five to report at the ____ ____."

to a committee · whole · no

F 123. If you wish to discuss the pending question informally and freely, you would stand and say, "I move that we consider the resolution as if in a ____ ____ ____ whole."

refer · committee · next meeting

F 124. The next subsidiary motion, to amend a motion, has been discussed previously in Set D. The motion to amend ranks after the motions to refer in the order of ____.

committee of the

F 125.   Let's briefly review the motion to
_____, change, or modify, another motion.

precedence

F 126.   When we _____ another motion, we
change it in some way. There are two degrees
of amendments: (1) first _____ and (2) _____
_____. (See *Robert's Rules of Order Newly
Revised*, pages 108-140.)

amend

F 127.   An amendment must be germane to
the *subject* it is amending. This means that the
amendment must relate to the same _____ as
the motion being amended.

*amend · degree ·
second degree*

F 128.   If this motion is vague in your mind,
go back and review Set D to refresh yourself
on how to _____ a motion.

subject

F 129.   If a motion to refer to a committee is
on the floor being debated, would a motion
to amend the main motion be in order? Yes
or no?

amend

F 130.   The final subsidiary motion to be considered is to postpone indefinitely. This motion takes precedence only over main motions
and yields to all privileged, incidental, and
other subsidiary _____.

no

F 131.   If you want to do away with a motion and decrease the chances of its being
moved again, you would use the motion to
_____ indefinitely. (See *Robert's Rules of
Order Newly Revised*, pages 105-108.)

motions

F 132.   This motion is made by saying, "I
move that we _____ _____ the motion . . . ,"
stating the motion.

postpone

F 133.   The real object of this motion is not to postpone action on the motion but to reject the pending motion without voting on it. If we pass the motion to postpone the main question _____, then this main question is postponed for an indefinite period of time.

postpone indefinitely

F 134.   This subsidiary motion to _____ _____ is often used to give the opponents of a main question an idea as to their numerical strength. It can act for them as a straw vote on the main question.

indefinitely

F 135.   To postpone indefinitely also provides a means of disposing of a main _____ on which it may be embarrassing for the group to vote yes or no.

postpone indefinitely

F 136.   To _____ _____ also provides a way of disposing of an ill-advised motion.

motion or question

F 137.   A main motion that has been postponed _____ may not be renewed at the same meeting.

postpone indefinitely

F 138.   If we vote and pass to postpone indefinitely, the only way we can reintroduce the postponed motion is to make a completely new _____ during new business no sooner than the next regular business meeting.

indefinitely

F 139.   If a member moves to buy a pink elephant for the club mascot and will not withdraw his motion, then you could move to _____ _____ and, if passed, reduce the chances of this motion ever coming up again.

motion

F 140.   To postpone indefinitely does not suppress *debate* on the main question; there-

postpone indefinitely

fore, it allows more _____ on the subject of
the main question.

F 141.   To postpone indefinitely gives the
opponents of the main question an opportunity to kill it without actually voting on the
_____ motion.

debate

F 142.   If the opponents of the main motion
fail to pass the motion to postpone indefinitely, then the group has to vote on the
_____ motion.

main

F 143.   If you want to try to do away with a
motion and reduce its chances of coming up
again, what motion would you use?

main

F 144.   The subsidiary motion to postpone indefinitely takes precedence over _____
motions.

*postpone indefi-
nitely*

F 145.   Does the motion to amend take
precedence over the motion to postpone indefinitely? Yes or no?

main

F 146.   Do privileged motions take precedence
over the subsidiary motion to postpone indefinitely? Yes or no?

yes

F 147.   Does the motion to adjourn take precedence over the motion to amend? Yes or
no?

yes

F 148.   The subsidiary motions in their order
of precedence are;
1. lay on the _____
2. previous _____
3. _____ or _____ debate

yes

4. _____ definitely
5. _____ _____ _____ committee or _____ of the _____
6. _____ (change or alter a motion)
7. postpone _____

F 149.   The privileged motions in their order of precedence are:
1. to fix the _____ to which to adjourn
2. _____ (end a meeting)
3. _____ (temporarily take a break)
4. _____ _____ privilege
5. orders _____ _____ _____

1) table 2) question 3) limit · extend 4) postpone 5) refer to a · committee · whole 6) amend 7) indefinitely

F 150.   If you want to delay action on a motion until 6:30 on July 11, you would use the motion to _____ _____ _____ _____ _____.

1) time 2) adjourn 3) recess 4) question of 5) of the day

F 151.   Does postpone to a certain time take precedence over postpone indefinitely? Yes or no?

postpone to a certain time or postpone definitely

F 152.   Would a motion to move the previous question be in order while we are discussing whether to postpone indefinitely? Yes or no?

yes

F 153.   If you want the group to discuss the main motion informally, you would use the subsidiary motion of moving to a _____ _____ _____ _____.

yes

F 154.   If you want to have a group of three members investigate a main motion and report back to the group at the next meeting, you would move to _____ _____ _____ _____.

committee of the whole

F 155.   What are the four general classifications of motions?
1. _____ motions

refer to a committee

2. subsidiary ____
3. ____ motions
4. incidental ____

You are now ready to begin Set G, Main
Motions.

*1) privileged 2) mo-
tions 3) main 4)
motions*

set G

MAIN MOTIONS[1]

Place a card or piece of paper (approximately 3″ x 5″) over the page. Move the card down the page to expose one frame at a time. Read the frame carefully. The blanks in the frame indicate where essential information is missing; the number of blanks indicates the number of words in the desired response. Do not write in the blanks; write your response in the space to the right of the frame. Then move the card down to expose the next frame; as you do so you will also expose the correct answer to the previous frame, which is given in the right-hand column opposite the next frame. Check your answer before continuing the program.

G 1.   The next general classification of motions to be considered is that of main motions. These motions are the lowest in *precedence* of the four classifications of motions and do NOT have any order of _____ among themselves.

G 2.   The first kind of motion to be considered under this heading is the motion that proposes some new action to be taken up by the group and is the *main* vehicle by which business is brought before the group. These motions are called _____ motions (the same name as the general classification of this group of motions).

precedence

---

[1] For a more detailed discussion of this subject, see *Robert's Rules of Order Newly Revised*, pages 52 and 64–68.

G 3.   Unlike subsidiary and privileged motions, which have an order of precedence,
main motions do NOT have an order of ____.
Therefore, one main motion does not take
precedence over another.

main

G 4.   If one main motion is on the floor and
another main motion is made before the first
one is disposed of, the second main motion is
out of ____.

precedence

G 5.   If a main motion is on the floor being
debated and a member moves to amend this
main motion, the amendment would take
____ over the main motion and would have
to be disposed of before the main motion.
The motion to amend is a ____ motion, and
subsidiary motions take precedence over main
motions. If the amendment is passed, it would
affect the main motion in some way. (See
Robert's Rules of Order Newly Revised,
pages 82-104.)

order

G 6.   A main motion is a clear but brief
statement of a proposed action. The procedure used in making a motion is:
1. rise and face the chair
2. address the ____
3. await recognition of the chairman and
then make the motion
(See Set C for review of how to gain the
floor.)

*precedence · subsid-
iary*

G 7.   There are five motions that fall under
the classification of main motions. Since there
is NO order of precedence among main motions, it does not matter in what order they
are listed.
1. main ____
2. motion to reconsider
3. motion to rescind
4. motion to make a special order of business
5. motion to take from the table

chairman or chair

G 8.   Is there any order of precedence
among these five main motions? Yes or no?

motion

G 9.   The next motion to be considered
under the classification of main motions is
the motion to take from the table. The first
motion considered under *main* motions was a
_____ motion.

no

G 10.   Only a motion that has been laid on
the table can be taken from the _____. (See
Robert's Rules of Order Newly Revised,
pages 252-256.)

main

G 11.   When we take a motion from the
table, it means that previously the motion
was laid _____ _____ _____ or postponed temporarily by the group for more urgent business.

table

G 12.   A question is supposed to be laid on
the table only temporarily, with the expecta-
tion of resuming its consideration after the
disposal of the interrupting question. The motion to take _____ _____ _____ the previously
tabled motion would be in order immediately
after disposing of the interrupting question.

on the table

G 13.   To take a motion from the table
means that now we wish to _____ this motion
again.

from the table

G 14.   We can only take from the table motions that were placed on the _____ at an
earlier time.

consider or debate

G 15.   If we placed a motion on the table at
our last meeting and now during either new or
unfinished business we wish to debate this
motion further, we would say, "I move that

table

we ____ ____ ____ ____ the motion . . . ,"
stating the exact motion.

G 16.   If we want to take a motion from the
table at the same meeting or at some later
meeting, we would move to take the motion
____ ____ ____.

take from the table

G 17.   If a motion is tabled, the only way
this motion can be brought before the group
again is by moving, "I move that we ____
____ ____ ____. . . ."

from the table

G 18.   Can we move to take a motion from
the table during new business? Yes or no?

take from the table

G 19.   If you want to debate further a motion that has been set aside temporarily by
laying it on the table, you would move to
____ ____ ____ ____ this motion.

yes

G 20.   The next motion to be studied is called
the motion to reconsider. To reconsider deals
with changing the group's decision (vote) on a
main motion. To reconsider guards against
hasty action taken on ____ motions.

take from the table

G 21.   If you voted in *favor* of a motion and
it passed but later you want to change your
vote on that main motion, you can change it
by the motion to reconsider. In order for you
to make this motion, however, you must have
voted in ____ of the main motion and not
against it. (See *Robert's Rules of Order Newly Revised*, pages 265-284.)

main

G 22.   This motion to reconsider an action
taken earlier by the group gives the members
an opportunity to change their ____ if they
change their minds.

favor

G 23. In case you voted "yes" and the motion *failed*, then you would be out of order in
making the motion to reconsider the vote on
the main ____.

vote or decision

G 24. On each main motion there is an affirmative (yes) vote and negative (no) vote. If
the main motion passes, then we would assume the ____ votes were more than the negative votes.

motion

G 25. If the affirmative votes were more
than the negative votes and the motion passed,
then anyone voting affirmatively (yes) could
move to ____ the vote taken.

affirmative or yes

G 26. If you voted "yes" on a main motion
and the majority of other members voted
"no" and the motion lost, then you could
not move to ____ the motion because you
voted on the losing side.

reconsider

G 27. In order for you to move to reconsider,
you must have voted on the side that won the
decision on the main motion—commonly
called the *prevailing* side—and not on the ____
side, which did not win the vote.

reconsider

G 28. If the prevailing side (the side that
won) was the negative vote on a main motion,
then in order for you to move to ____ the
vote taken you must have voted "no" originally.

losing

G 29. The prevailing side is the side that
wins the decision, and it can be either the
____ or "no" votes.

reconsider

G 30. If a group votes 10 in favor and 9
against a main motion and the motion carries,

"yes"

which side is the prevailing side? The "yes" or "no" votes?

G 31.   If a group votes 10 in favor and 9 against a main motion and the motion passes, would you be in order in moving to reconsider if you voted against the motion? Yes or no?

"yes" votes

G 32.   If you were one of the members who voted against a main motion and the motion failed, would you be in order in moving to _____ the voting and change your vote from against to in favor? Yes or no?

no

G 33.   If a motion to reconsider is made, this should indicate that at least one person who voted on the prevailing side has changed his mind and wishes to change his _____.

reconsider · yes

G 34.   The motion to reconsider relates only to the vote taken and not to the relevant motion itself. If the motion to _____ carries, debate is reopened as if no vote had been taken on the relevant matter.

vote

G 35.   When we reconsider a vote, we are dealing only with the _____ taken and not with the motion on which we voted.

reconsider

G 36.   The first rule to remember about the motion to reconsider is that the maker must have voted on the _____ side. A second rule is that this motion must be made at the same meeting or on the day following the original vote.

vote

G 37.   The motion to reconsider must be taken either at the same meeting or on the following day for it to be in _____. Otherwise, this motion would be out of order, and it

prevailing or winning

would not matter whether the members had
changed their minds or not.

G 38. To make the motion to reconsider,
you would simply say, "I move to ⎯⎯ the
action taken by this group on . . . ," stating
the main motion.

order

G 39. The chairman may and should ask a
person moving to reconsider a main motion,
"Did you vote on the ⎯⎯ side?" If he did,
he would answer "yes," and the motion
would be in order.

reconsider

G 40. If the chairman asks you, "Did you
vote on the prevailing side?" and you answer
"no," then the chairman would rule you out
of order, and the motion to ⎯⎯ would be
disregarded.

prevailing

G 41. This motion to ⎯⎯, or to change the
vote on a motion, is very complicated. It cannot be applied to certain motions, and, if
adopted, it has various effects. (For further
discussion of this motion, see *Robert's Rules
of Order Newly Revised*, pages 267-270.)

reconsider

G 42. The motion to reconsider relates to
the ⎯⎯ taken on a motion. The next motion to be studied relates to the motion rather
than to the vote. This motion is called the
motion to rescind.

reconsider

G 43. To *rescind* means to cancel. If an organization wishes to void a motion previously
passed, it can do so by the motion to ⎯⎯.
(See *Robert's Rules of Order Newly Revised*,
pages 256-260.)

vote

G 44. You would be in order in moving to

rescind

rescind a vote taken at a previous meeting
without having voted on the _____ side (the
side that won).

G 45. To rescind is not in order at the same
meeting that the original vote was taken. If
you wish to move to _____ action on a main
motion, you must make this motion at a following meeting.

prevailing

G 46. If the group voted today to buy a
Great Dane as a club mascot and you want to
rescind this motion, you must wait until the
_____ meeting to make this motion.

rescind

G 47. If the motion to _____ is passed, it
nullifies the motion itself.

following or next

G 48. The motion to rescind should not be
made if one wishes to change the vote on a
motion because the motion to reconsider
deals with the _____ on a motion.

rescind

G 49. To rescind means to cancel or nullify
the whole motion. This motion is not in order
at the same meeting at which the original vote
was taken, but it is in order at any meeting
_____ the meeting at which the vote was taken.

vote

G 50. If the motion to rescind passes, the
relevant motion is canceled; but if the motion
fails, the relevant motion is not _____.

following or after

G 51. If you wish to move to rescind a motion passed at a previous meeting, you would
say, "I move to _____ the action taken on . . .
(stating the motion) at . . . (giving the meeting)."

canceled

G 52.   Now for a quick review. To _____ *rescind*
means to cancel a motion. To reconsider the
action taken by the group means at least one
person who voted on the prevailing side
wishes to change his _____ on the motion.

G 53.   You can move to *cancel* the action of *rescind · vote*
the group on a main motion without having
voted on the prevailing side by moving to
_____ the main motion previously passed by
the group.

G 54.   If you voted on the prevailing side *rescind*
(the side that won the decision) but you want
to *cancel* the action taken by the group rather
than just change the vote, what motion would
you make? Rescind or reconsider?

G 55.   If the club passes a motion to buy a *rescind*
new flag and you voted against this motion,
would you be out of order in moving to reconsider? Yes or no? Why (in your own
words)?

G 56.   At this *same* meeting and under the *yes · you must have*
same circumstances, would you be out of *voted on the prevail-*
order in moving to rescind the action taken *ing side in order to*
to buy the new flag? Yes or no? Why (in your *move to reconsider*
own words)?

G 57.   The motions to change decisions are: *yes · you cannot*
1. _____ (if you voted on the prevailing side) *move to rescind at*
2. _____ (cancel a motion passed at a previous *the same meeting*
meeting) *that the motion was*
made and voted on

G 58.   We have previously discussed the call *reconsider · rescind*
for the orders of the day and the motion to
postpone definitely (to a certain time). These
two motions correspond closely to the next
motion included under the classification of

main _____, the motion to make a special
order of business. (See *Robert's Rules of
Order Newly Revised*, pages 209-218.)

G 59.   Remember that when the motion is
passed to postpone definitely a particular
question, that question does not automatically
become a special order unless it is explicitly
stated that it be made a _____ order. (See
frames F55-F71 for review of the motion to
postpone definitely.)

motions

G 60.   The orders of the day may be called in
order to discuss a motion that was postponed
definitely or made a special order of _____.

special

G 61.   To make a _____ _____ of business temporarily changes the regular order of business.

business

G 62.   We can use the motion special order
of business to set a *special* time to consider a
_____ question.

special order

G 63.   To make a special order of business
means that the group wishes to consider a
question out of the regular order of _____ but
still within the rules of parliamentary procedure and the organization.

special

G 64.   If your club meets at 7:00 p.m. and
you want to consider the problem of lack of
members at 7:30, then you would say, "I
move that we make 'lack of members' a special _____ _____ _____ at 7:30."

business

G 65.   If the club votes to discuss lack of
members at 7:30, then at that hour the president will announce that "lack of members"
will be discussed—even if the club is discussing

order of business

another subject at the time—because the club
had previously passed the motion to make a
____ ____ ____ ____ of this subject at 7:30.

G 66.   To make a special order of business
ensures the discussion of a subject at a ____
time or place during the regular order of
business.

*special order of
business*

G 67.   We studied earlier the eight steps in
the order of business. The motion ____ ____
of business allows an organization to deviate
from this regular order of business in order to
discuss a subject at a specific time or place.

*special, specific,
given, etc.*

G 68.   Review your understanding of the
material in this set by completing the following statements:
1. The ____ ____ is the main vehicle by
which business is brought before the group.
2. Main motions have no order of ____
among themselves.
3. If you wish to consider a question which
was temporarily laid aside for consideration
of more urgent business, you would use the
motion to ____ ____ ____ ____.
4. In order to make a motion to reconsider,
you must have voted on the ____ side.
5. If an organization wishes to void a motion
previously passed, it can do so by the motion
to ____.
6. You can use the motion ____ ____ ____
____ to set a special time to consider a special
question.

special order

You are now ready to begin Set H, Incidental
Motions.

*1) main motion 2)
precedence 3) take
from the table 4)
prevailing or win-
ning 5) rescind 6)
special order of
business*

set H

INCIDENTAL MOTIONS[1]

Place a card or piece of paper (approximately 3″ x 5″) over the page. Move the card down the page to expose one frame at a time. Read the frame carefully. The blanks in the frame indicate where essential information is missing; the number of blanks indicates the number of words in the desired response. Do not write in the blanks; write your response in the space to the right of the frame. Then move the card down to expose the next frame; as you do so you will also expose the correct answer to the previous frame, which is given in the right-hand column opposite the next frame. Check your answer before continuing the program.

H 1.   We have now covered three of the four general classifications of motions. The three general classifications already studied are: (1) privileged motions, (2) subsidiary motions, and (3) _____ motions. The fourth classification is that of *incidental motions*.

H 2.   *Incidental* motions are motions that are _____ to a question pending before the group and should be decided before any other business is taken up.

main

H 3.   Incidental motions arise out of another question that is pending and there-

incidental

---

[1] For a more detailed discussion of this subject, see *Robert's Rules of Order Newly Revised*, pages 58–64.

fore take _____ over the motion to which they
are incidental and must be decided first.

H 4.   Privileged motions take precedence
over all other classes of motions but may
yield this precedence to incidental _____ when
an incidental motion is legitimately incidental
to a privileged motion. (See *Robert's Rules of
Order Newly Revised*, page 62.)

precedence

H 5.   In order for an incidental motion to
take precedence over a certain motion, it must
be legitimately incidental to that motion.
Thus, incidental _____ can take precedence
over subsidiary motions.

motions

H 6.   There is NO order of _____ among the
incidental motions.

motions

H 7.   The first _____ motion to be discussed
is point of order. (See *Robert's Rules of
Order Newly Revised*, pages 212-218.)

precedence

H 8.   To make a point of order means to
bring some error of procedure to the attention of the chair and other members so that
it can be corrected. This allows changes in
order of _____ during the meetings.

incidental

H 9.   To make a point of order, you rise and
state, "I rise to a point of _____." The chairman replies, "State your point," and then you
report the procedural error.

*procedure or
business*

H 10.   If discussion on a main motion is out
of order, a member may rise and make the
motion, "I rise to a _____ _____ _____."

order

H 11.   If the chairman does not call for the

point of order

votes in favor of a motion but only for those
opposed to the motion, a member may ____
____ ____ ____ ____ ____ and remind the
chairman of his failure to call for the affirmative votes.

H 12. If a member stands and starts to talk
without being recognized by the chair, you
may ____ ____ ____ ____ ____ ____ and
note the correct procedure.

rise to a point of order

H 13. Generally, a point of order is made by
saying, "I ____ to a ____ ____ ____."

rise to a point of order

H 14. If the chairman thinks your point of
order is well taken, the procedure is corrected.
If he does not think it is ____ ____, the order
of business proceeds without correction.

rise · point of order

H 15. If the chairman says, "Five voted to
adjourn, six voted not to adjourn, and a simple
majority is needed, therefore we are adjourned," you could rise to a ____ ____ ____
and note the incorrect procedure of the
chairman.

well taken

H 16. To correct a breach in the order of
procedure or a wrong decision by the chairman, you would make a ____ ____ ____.

point of order

H 17. If the chairman does not think your
point is ____ ____, the group may overrule
the chairman's decision by using another
motion—appeal from the decision of the chair.

point of order

H 18. If your point ____ ____ is not accept-
ed by the chairman but it is the correct procedure, you may appeal from the decision of
the chair, which is the next incidental motion.
(See *Robert's Rules of Order Newly Revised*,
pages 218-222.)

well taken

H 19.   To appeal from the decision of the chair means to override a decision made by the chairman. It is like the U.S. Senate overriding the President's veto of a bill. You would make the appeal by saying, "I ＿＿＿ from the decision of the chair."

of order

H 20.   It must be remembered that the power of the chairman is limited only by the power given him by the ＿＿＿ of an organization.

appeal

H 21.   If the members disapprove of the chairman's decision on a motion, they may appeal from ＿＿＿ ＿＿＿ ＿＿＿ ＿＿＿ ＿＿＿.

members

H 22.   To make the motion to appeal from the decision of the chair, you would say, "I ＿＿＿ ＿＿＿ ＿＿＿ ＿＿＿ ＿＿＿ ＿＿＿ ＿＿＿." If this motion is seconded, the chair should state clearly the question at issue.

the decision of the chair

H 23.   After your motion to appeal from the ＿＿＿ ＿＿＿ ＿＿＿ ＿＿＿ has been seconded, the chairman will say, "The chair's decision has been appealed from."

appeal from the decision of the chair

H 24.   If an appeal is made, the chair will say, "The chair's decision has been ＿＿＿ from; all those in favor of sustaining the chair's decision raise your hands" . . . "all those opposed raise your hands."

decision of the chair

H 25.   Suppose there are 5 votes for and 4 votes against a motion that needs a two-thirds vote to pass and the chair says, "The motion carries (passes)." If you rise to a point of order and the chair rules you out of order, what motion could you now make to keep the chairman from making the wrong decision? (Write out the motion.)

appealed

H 26.   The chair's decision is the same as a vote by the chairman. When you appeal ____ ____ ____ ____ ____, you are saying, "I think we should all have an equal 'vote' on this matter."

I appeal from the decision of the chair.

H 27.   Only a simple majority is needed to sustain a decision of the chair. If there is a tie vote by the members, the chair's decision is sustained because his decision is also classified as a vote, which gives the ____ majority necessary to sustain the decision.

from the decision of the chair

H 28.   If a chairman makes a decision you do not like, you would appeal from ____ ____ ____ ____ ____. This motion is in order every time the chairman makes a decision.

simple

H 29.   An appeal from the decision of the chair is another motion that must be decided on as it is raised, and it is in order every time the ____ makes a decision for the group without letting the group vote on the matter.

the decision of the chair

H 30.   The next incidental motion is to suspend the rules. The first two incidental motions were:
1. point ____ ____
2. appeal ____ ____ ____ ____ ____ ____

chair or chairman

H 31.   To suspend the *rules* is used to set aside temporarily the regular ____ governing the organization. We can NOT suspend the constitution and by-laws, only the standing rules of an organization. (See *Robert's Rules of Order Newly Revised*, pages 222-227.)

1) of order 2) from the decision of the chair

H 32.   In order to dispose of a special bit of business which is against the rules of an organization, we would move to ____ the rules.

rules

H 33. If you have a very important item of business that you want brought before the group at some time earlier than the designated time, you would move to ___ ___ ___ .

suspend

H 34. To suspend ___ ___ is different from making a special order of business in that suspending the rules allows you to take up some business that is against the standing rules of the organization.

suspend the rules

H 35. The main motion to make a special order of business is generally used to designate a future time and date when a question will be discussed. The motion to ___ the rules is used in order to do something that the standing rules of the organization would normally not allow.

the rules

H 36. Thus to suspend the rules and to make a special order of business differ in that to suspend ___ ___ refers to setting aside temporarily the rules of an organization that would make it impossible to consider a particular question.

suspend

H 37. You could move to suspend the rules in order to bring up a special item of business which otherwise would be out of ___ .

the rules

H 38. When you move to suspend the ___ , it could mean that you have something important to discuss that cannot wait until later.

order

H 39. When you move to ___ ___ ___ , you must specify the object for the suspension, and only that object will be considered if the motion passes.

rules

H 40. The fourth incidental ___ to be con-

suspend the rules

sidered is the motion which allows a member
to object to consideration of a question moved
by another member. (See *Robert's Rules of
Order Newly Revised*, pages 227-229.)

H 41.   If you do not think a motion that has   *motion*
been made is worth *consideration* by the
group, you can object to _____.

H 42.   In order to express your objection to   *consideration*
discussing a particular motion, you would say,
"I object _____ _____ of this motion."

H 43.   You would object to consideration if   *to consideration*
you think the motion made is irrelevant, ob-
jectionable, or unworthy of the members'
time and thus you do not want it _____.

H 44.   If a motion is not in the best interest   *considered, debated,*
of the group, you could use the incidental   *or discussed*
motion _____ _____ _____ of the motion.

H 45.   If a person makes a motion that is un-   *object to consider-*
important or is not related to the business of   *ation*
the meeting, you could _____ _____ _____.

H 46.   To object to consideration has special   *object to consider-*
qualifications in that it must be made right   *ation*
after the second and before debate begins on
a motion. Therefore, to _____ _____ _____
affects the status and debate of a motion.

H 47.   You must object to consideration of a   *object to consider-*
motion prior to any debate on it or you will   *ation*
be out of _____.

H 48.   The motion object _____ _____ must   *order*
be made right after the main motion is sec-
onded and before debate begins.

H 49. When is the motion object to consideration in order?
1. after the second and before debate
2. before the second
3. after debate has been started

to consideration

H 50. You can give or refuse to give your reason for objecting ____ ____.

1

H 51. If you are asked to give your reason for objecting, you may state your reason or you may ____ to give your reason.

to consideration

H 52. If someone asks you why you object to a motion, you have the privilege of either giving or refusing to give your reason. True or false?

refuse

H 53. What are the two ways you can answer a person who has asked you why you object to consideration? (In your own words.)

true

H 54. To ____ ____ ____ enables an organization to avoid altogether any question that may be considered irrelevant, objectionable, or unworthy of the members' time and consideration.

1) give your reason
2) refuse to give
your reason

H 55. Another incidental motion is the call for a division. A call for a division means that we wish to check the results of a voice "yes-no" vote by having the voters give a standing vote for and ____ the question. (See *Robert's Rules of Order Newly Revised*, pages 237-239.)

object to consideration

H 56. A call for a ____ may be made without obtaining the floor. When a division is called, the chair will proceed to take the vote again, this time by having the affirmative rise

against

and then, when they are seated, by having the
negative rise.

H 57. Of course, a division is called when
you have already had a voice vote or when
you are in doubt about the number voting
and you wish to check the voting by having
the members _____.

division

H 58. The call _____ _____ _____ is made by
simply saying, "I call for a division," or "I
doubt the vote," or "Division."

stand

H 59. An extreme version of this call for a
_____ would be to actually divide the members
of the assembly as if choosing up sides. All
those in favor of the motion would rise and
go to one side of the room; all those against
would rise and go to the other side. Remember, this is the extreme way.

for a division

H 60. There may be times during a meeting
when members wish to obtain information
concerning the rules of parliamentary procedure, ask questions of the speaker, or make
some other pertinent *request.* Two motions
that enable members to _____ such information are parliamentary inquiry and point of
information.

division

H 61. The first motion, *parliamentary* inquiry, enables a member who is not quite
clear on _____ law to gain enlightenment on a
point.

request or obtain

H 62. By requesting a parliamentary inquiry,
a member is able to find out the correct procedure during a meeting. Therefore, a parliamentary inquiry can take _____ over all motions. (See *Robert's Rules of Order Newly
Revised,* pages 243-251.)

parliamentary

H 63.   If you do not know the correct procedure to follow, you may ask the chairman for a _____ inquiry in order to find out.

precedence

H 64.   Every member of an organization should have a working knowledge of parliamentary procedure, but if a point is in doubt, it is best to consult the chairman, parliamentarian, or a reference book by requesting a parliamentary _____.

parliamentary

H 65.   The parliamentary inquiry enables any member to seek advice about the correct _____ procedure to follow.

inquiry

H 66.   The incidental motion that allows a member to find out the correct parliamentary procedure to follow is the _____ _____.

parliamentary

H 67.   To request a parliamentary inquiry, you would say, "I rise to a _____ _____"; the chairman would then ask you to state your inquiry.

parliamentary
inquiry

H 68.   Any point of order may be preceded or followed by a _____ inquiry if the correct procedure is in doubt.

parliamentary
inquiry

H 69.   If a parliamentary _____ interrupts a speaker and there is no reason to answer it until the speaker has closed his remarks, then the answer may wait until the speaker is finished.

parliamentary

H 70.   The second motion that enables a member to gain *information* is the motion called point of _____.

inquiry

H 71.   A _____ _____ _____ relating to the

information

pending business is treated just as a parliamentary _____. (See *Robert's Rules of Order
Newly Revised*, pages 243-251.)

H 72.   The motion point of information enables a member to find out additional information about the subject being debated.
Therefore, _____ _____ _____ takes precedence
over all motions.

*point of information
· inquiry*

H 73.   The motion point of information is
very useful in that it enables a member to
request additional _____ about a subject being
discussed.

point of information

H 74.   A point of information is similar to a
parliamentary _____; a point of information
allows a member to ask questions concerning
any pending business, whereas a parliamentary
inquiry allows a member to ask questions
about the parliamentary procedure to be used.

information

H 75.   The point of information is directed
to the chairman. If the chairman can answer
the point, he should do so; however, if the
_____ cannot answer the question, he may
direct the question to a member of the organization for an answer.

inquiry

H 76.   If one member has the floor and is
talking and another member wants to ask the
speaker a question concerning his speech, he
could ask, "Will the speaker yield to a question?" This is the same as using the motion
point _____ _____.

chairman

H 77.   If the speaker on the floor will yield
to a question, then the member making the
request for _____ will ask the question; if not,
the member making the _____ _____ _____ will

of information

have to sit down and the speaker will continue.

H 78. In case the speaker on the floor does yield to the question, the question should be directed to the *chairman*, and the answer should be directed to the _____ also. This procedure does not allow one member of the organization to argue directly with another.

information ∘ point of information

H 79. The final incidental motion to be studied is the motion to withdraw a motion. The originator of a motion may move to withdraw his _____ any time before the voting on the question has commenced. (See *Robert's Rules of Order Newly Revised*, pages 246-248.)

chairman

H 80. The motion to withdraw a motion is in order at any time during the debate on a main motion and can be moved only by the person who made the main _____ being debated.

motion

H 81. It should be emphasized that this motion, withdraw a motion, is in order any time during the debate on a main motion, but only the _____ of the main motion can move to withdraw the motion.

motion

H 82. If you make a motion, you may move to withdraw your motion during the debate on it by saying, "I move to _____ my motion . . . ," stating the motion.

maker or originator

H 83. Only the maker of the motion can make the incidental motion to withdraw the _____ .

withdraw

H 84. The maker of a motion may request to withdraw his _____ if he changes his mind

motion

after it has been made, seconded, and opened
for debate.

H 85.   If you make a motion and while it is
being debated you change your mind and wish
to withdraw it, you would say, "I move to
_____ _____ motion . . . ," stating the motion.

motion

H 86.   We studied earlier that once a motion
was made, seconded, and restated by the
chairman, that motion became the property
of the whole _____ or all the members of the
organization.

withdraw the

H 87.   The maker of a motion is the only
person who can request to withdraw his motion but another member may request the
original mover to withdraw the motion. Once
the group begins debating the motion, however, the group must give its consent before
the motion is _____.

organization, group,
club, etc.

H 88.   If someone objects to the maker's
withdrawing his motion, then the members
must cast their _____ to see if the group will
consent to letting the motion be withdrawn.

withdrawn

H 89.   The person who seconded the motion
does not have to agree with the maker of the
motion in order for the maker to _____ his
motion.

votes

H 90.   Can the person who seconded the
maker's motion request to withdraw the motion? Yes or no?

withdraw

H 91.   If a person objects to your withdrawing your motion, the group must _____ to give
you permission to withdraw it.

no

H 92.   If there is a fault in the procedure during the debate on a motion to postpone definitely or any motion pending or being considered, would it be in order to rise to a point of order? Yes or no?

vote

H 93.   If an irrelevant and objectionable motion is made, what incidental motion would you use after the second and before debate to stop action on the motion?

yes

H 94.   If a motion you made is now being debated and you change your mind and wish to cancel the motion, what motion would you use to stop any further discussion?

object to consideration

H 95.   If you want to ask a question of a member discussing an issue, you would say, "I rise to a point of _____. Will the speaker yield to a question?"

withdraw the motion

H 96.   If you are in doubt about a point of parliamentary procedure, you could say, "I rise for a _____ inquiry."

information

H 97.   If the chairman makes a decision the group does not like, you would appeal _____ _____ _____ of the chair in order to attempt to override his decision.

parliamentary

H 98.   If someone makes a motion that is out of line with the business of the group, you could move to _____ _____ consideration of the question.

from the decision

H 99.   If a motion you made is now being debated and you change your mind and want to cancel the motion, you would move to _____ _____ _____ .

object to

H 100.   Can you move the previous question
while a point of order is being discussed? Yes
or no?

withdraw the motion

H 101.   If you are in doubt about what the
procedure should be, would you be in order
to rise for a parliamentary inquiry when a motion to adjourn is on the floor? Yes or no?

no

H 102.   Can the maker of a main motion move
to withdraw his motion when this main motion has been amended and the group is debating the *amendment?* Yes or no?

no

H 103.   If there is an error in procedure, you
would say, "I rise to a _____ _____ _____."

no

H 104.   Review your knowledge of the information in this set by completing the following
statements:
1. _____ _____ are motions which are incidental to a question and should be decided before
any other business is taken up.
2. If you disapprove of the chairman's decision on a motion, you may appeal _____ _____

_____ _____ _____ _____.
3. The motion to _____ _____ _____ allows a
group to take up some business that is against
the standing rules of the organization.
4. To bring a procedural error to the attention of the chairman you would make a _____

_____ _____.
5. If you think a motion that has been made
is unworthy of consideration by the group,
you can _____ _____ _____:
6. The _____ _____ enables a member to seek
advice about the correct parliamentary procedure to follow.

point of order

You are now ready to begin Set I, Officers and Elections.

1) incidental motions 2) from the decision of the chair 3) suspend the rules 4) point of order 5) object to consideration 6) parliamentary inquiry

set 1

OFFICERS AND ELECTIONS[1]

Place a card or piece of paper (approximately 3″ x 5″) over the page. Move the card down the page to expose one frame at a time. Read the frame carefully. The blanks in the frame indicate where essential information is missing; the number of blanks indicates the number of words in the desired response. Do not write in the blanks; write your response in the space to the right of the frame. Then move the card down to expose the next frame; as you do so you will also expose the correct answer to the previous frame, which is given in the right-hand column opposite the next frame. Check your answer before continuing the program.

I 1.   So far we have referred to the leader of an organization as the chairman. He is also often called the president. The president, therefore, is usually the _____ of an organization.

I 2.   The president is the senior officer and presides over all meetings held by the _____.

chairman

I 3.   Although we have referred to him as the chairman, the senior officer of an organization is also known as the _____.

organization or members

I 4.   It is the president's responsibility to serve the members of the _____.

president

[1] For a more detailed discussion of this subject, see *Robert's Rules of Order Newly Revised*, pages 368–389.

I 5.   It is also the president's responsibility to create the atmosphere for cooperative deliberation. To do this he must encourage the members to participate in the activities of the ____.

organization

I 6.   To encourage participation by the members, the president must be sure the members are informed and interested in the ____ being discussed.

organization

I 7.   The president should know and understand the members of the organization in order to encourage their ____ during the meeting.

subject, motion, or topic

I 8.   The president is actually responsible for seeing that *worthwhile* deliberations take place at each meeting. Consideration of any subject connected with the proper business of the meeting is considered ____.

participation or interest

I 9.   Discussion may arise about any subject the ____ of an organization consider worthwhile.

worthwhile

I 10.   If worthwhile business takes place in a meeting and the meeting progresses rapidly and effectively, then the ____ is doing his job well.

members

I 11.   The president can favor no one but must preside impersonally and impartially. This means that he must give the same attention and fairness to each ____ of the organization.

president or chairman

I 12.   In presiding impersonally, the president will never state his opinion on the ____ being discussed.

member

I 13. The president acts as an umpire or referee for the group. This means that he only keeps order and does not state his _____ on the subject being discussed.

subject, motion, or question

I 14. If for some reason the president is required to or wishes to speak on a subject, he must let someone else (the vice-president) preside. Then he speaks just as any other _____ would.

opinion

I 15. To be able to speak in a meeting, what must the president do? (In your own words.)

member

I 16. The chairman is also impersonal in referring to himself as "the chair" and not as "I." He refers to the members by name, but he calls himself "_____ _____."

He must let someone else preside for him before he may speak.

I 17. There are many things the chairman must be, but the most important is that he must be interested in the welfare of the _____ that has elected him its president.

the chair

I 18. The senior officer of an organization is called the _____.

organization

I 19. The person responsible for encouraging participation and keeping order in meetings is called the _____.

president or chairman

I 20. The president has many duties. One duty is to announce the steps in the order of _____ as they come due.

president or chairman

I 21. It might be a good idea for the president to prepare an outline of the eight steps in the order of business to guide him as he presides over the _____.

business

I 22.   When it is time for the first step in the order of business, the president will say, "The meeting will please come to ____."

meeting

I 23.   After the meeting has been called to order, the president will say, "The secretary will read the ____ of the last ____."

order

I 24.   After the reading and approval of the minutes, the president will ask, "Are there any reports from the ____ committees?"

minutes · meeting

I 25.   After the standing committee reports have been given, the president will ask, "Are there reports from the ____ ____?"

standing

I 26.   After the special committee reports have been given, but before taking up new business, the president will call for ____ business.

special committees

I 27.   After the unfinished business has been taken care of, the president will call for ____ business.

unfinished or old

I 28.   The next step is for the president to ask if there are any ____. This is the time to announce committee meetings, special thanks to someone, etc.

new

I 29.   The final step is for the president to ask if there is a motion that the meeting ____.

announcements

I 30.   Another duty of the president is to give the floor to members who address the chair. When a member addresses the chair, the chair will give him the ____ by recognizing him.

adjourn

I 31.   Each time a member wishes to speak
he must address the chair. He must then be
_____ by the president before he may speak.

floor

I 32.   Before a member can speak or make a
motion the chairman must _____ him.

recognized

I 33.   After the proposer of the motion has
had his turn to speak, the chairman should attempt to recognize alternately members from
both sides of the question being debated. That
is, he should try to give the floor to a person
speaking against the question, then a person
speaking _____ the proposal, and then against,
then for, etc., until debate ends.

recognize

I 34.   In recognizing members, the chairman
should give precedence to a *member* who has
not spoken on the motion over a _____ who
has already _____.

for

I 35.   By recognizing only one member at a
time, the president will prevent confusion and
give each member a chance to _____ without
interruption.

member • spoken

I 36.   After a motion has been made, the
president should restate the motion to be sure
it is understood before it is debated and _____
on.

speak or talk

I 37.   The president (chairman) sees that all
motions and questions arising in a *meeting* are
properly presented and debated. In short, he
sees that the business in each _____ is carried
on efficiently.

voted

I 38.   The president (together with the parliamentarian) will decide questions of parliamentary _____.

meeting

I 39.   The president must have a good knowledge of parliamentary procedure in order to decide questions arising among the ____.

procedure or inquiry

I 40.   The president might wish to refer to a good parliamentary procedure *manual* for answers to difficult questions. He should never hesitate to use the ____ if he is in doubt.

members

I 41.   One of the most useful manuals for reference is *Robert's Rules of Order Newly Revised.* It is a comprehensive manual and will no doubt answer many of the more difficult ____.

manual

I 42.   *Robert's Rules of Order Newly Revised* is a comprehensive ____ of parliamentary procedure.

questions

I 43.   If the president needs a good reference manual to answer difficult parliamentary procedure questions, he should consult ____ ____ ____ ____ ____ ____.

manual

I 44.   Although the president may wish to use a manual for the more difficult questions, he cannot be constantly referring to a book for his parliamentary ____.

Robert's Rules of Order Newly Revised

I 45.   The president can vote on any question, but he should use discretion because of the status of his position. Usually the president votes only to make or break a tie or when the ____ is by secret ballot.

procedure

I 46.   The president can vote to make or break a ____.

vote

I 47.   The president of an organization can vote on any ____, but generally he votes only

tie

to _____ or _____ a tie vote of the members or when there is a secret ballot.

I 48.   The president is not _____ to vote but may do so if he wishes.

question or motion ·
make · break

I 49.   If there is a tie on a motion requiring a simple majority and the president elects *not* to vote, then the motion remains a tie and therefore _____ to pass.

required

I 50.   If the votes taken on a motion are 10 affirmative and 10 negative, the president can pass the motion by voting on the _____ side.

fails

I 51.   If the votes taken on a motion are 21 affirmative and 20 negative, the president can defeat the motion by voting on the _____ side, thus making the vote a _____.

affirmative

I 52.   If the votes taken are 21 affirmative and 20 negative and the president does not wish to vote, then the motion is _____.

negative · tie

I 53.   As we have seen, the president may vote in a meeting to _____ or _____ a tie. He is never _____ to vote but may do so if he wishes.

passed

I 54.   The president is the leader of the organization, but this role does not mean that he controls the business of the organization. He is not elected to persuade the members to follow his *ideas* but, instead, to direct the members in carrying out their own _____.

make · break ·
required

I 55.   The president is not elected to carry out his own *wishes and desires* but, rather, to carry out the _____ _____ _____ of the members.

ideas

I 56.   Another officer in an organization is the vice-president. His chief duty is to be prepared to take charge in the absence of the _____.

wishes and desires

I 57.   When the vice-president acts in the place of the president, he has all the powers of that office. In the president's absence the vice-president will have the same duties that are designated for the _____.

president

I 58.   If the president wishes to speak on a particular subject during a meeting, the _____ might take over the chair.

president

I 59.   In addition to being prepared to replace or relieve the president, the _____ will usually serve as head of one of the important committees.

vice-president

I 60.   One of the traditional duties of the vice-president is to head one of the important _____ in the organization.

vice-president

I 61.   A third officer in an organization is the secretary. He acts as an assistant to the president and records the activities of each meeting in the form of minutes. In the absence of the president and vice-president, the _____ will preside.

committees

I 62.   The secretary keeps a written record of the meetings in the form of _____.

secretary

I 63.   After being approved, the minutes become a permanent record of the organization's activities. They are kept on file as an objective account of exactly what happened at the _____.

minutes

I 64.   The first items recorded in the minutes are the name of the organization and the
date, time, and place where the _____ was held.

meeting

I 65.   After this essential information has
been given, the minutes will be written in
paragraph form and "among other things" will
include each main motion that was made, with
the name of the person who made the _____.

meeting

I 66.   Every main motion that is made will
be recorded in the minutes along with the
name of the person making the motion. This
must be done accurately because these minutes will become a permanent _____ of the
organization's activities.

motion

I 67.   The secretary—and sometimes the
president—will sign his name at the end of the
_____.

record

I 68.   The minutes of a meeting will always
include every main motion that is made along
with the _____ of the person making it. Motions other than main motions are included if
they are considered pertinent and relevant to
future _____.

minutes

I 69.   The minutes will also include the time,
date, and _____ of the meeting.

name · meetings

I 70.   What items does the secretary record
in the minutes? List them.

place

I 71.   The secretary is responsible for all the
records of the organization and must be able
to produce them when requested by the officers or _____.

*name of the organi-
zation · time, date,
place of the meeting ·
all main motions ·
name of the maker
of each motion*

I 72.   There are certain records that the secretary must have at each meeting. One is a roll
of all members and another is a list of all committees. The president may wish to ask for a
roll call of the members, or he may want to
see the names of the members of a certain
_____.

members

I 73.   The secretary needs to have a roll of
all members and a record of all _____ members
with him at each meeting.

committee

I 74.   The secretary should also have a copy
of the organization's constitution and by-laws
with him at the meetings. The president may
ask the secretary to read an article from the
organization's _____ _____ _____.

committee

I 75.   The third item that the secretary
should have available at each meeting is a manual of parliamentary procedure. As we mentioned before, one of the best manuals on
parliamentary procedure is _____ _____ _____
_____ _____ _____.

*constitution and
by-laws*

I 76.   This manual should be available for
use by the members if they have a question
about the _____ _____ being used.

*Robert's Rules of
Order Newly
Revised*

I 77.   We have learned that the secretary
should have at least *three* records or documents available at each meeting. List them.

*parliamentary
procedure*

I 78.   The vice-president and the secretary
are members of the organization and may
make motions, debate, and vote just as any
other member. The only officer who cannot
make motions and debate in his official position is the _____.

*1) manual of parlia-
mentary procedure
2) constitution and
by-laws 3) roll of
members and com-
mittees*

I 79.   We have learned that the senior officer and chairman of an organization is the _____.

president or chairman

I 80.   The officer who takes the chair when the president is absent is the _____.

president

I 81.   Another officer, the _____, is the keeper of the organization's records.

vice-president

I 82.   The detailed procedure for the election of officers will be found in the organization's constitution and by-laws. The procedure, therefore, will vary from organization to _____.

secretary

I 83.   Although a few fundamental procedures concerning elections hold true in most organizations, the detailed procedure will be outlined in the organization's ____ ____ ____.

organization

I 84.   A few weeks before the time to elect new officers, the president will appoint a *nominating* committee. This committee is given the responsibility of _____ a person for each office in the organization.

constitution and by-laws

I 85.   The _____ committee will bring a list of suggested officers' names to the election meeting.

nominating or naming

I 86.   The president will call for a report from the nominating committee during either special committee reports or during new business. When called upon, the chairman of the ____ ____ will give the committee's report.

nominating

I 87.   The nominating committee will give its report either during special committee reports or during ____ ____.

nominating committee

I 88.   After the reading of the nominating committee's report, the president will ask if anyone present wishes to make a further nomination. Any member present may then stand and ____ a person for an office.

new business

I 89.   Many times a small club will not have a nominating committee, and all of the nominations will have to come from the ____ present at the meeting.

nominate

I 90.   When there is no nominating committee, nominations are taken from the floor—either as a special order of business or under new ____.

members

I 91.   If a member wishes to make a nomination for president from the floor, he would simply say, "I ____ John Doe for president."

business

I 92.   A second is not needed when a nomination has been made. The president accepts each name nominated and will allow the members to vote on each of the ____.

nominate

I 93.   If you wish to nominate Jane Smith for secretary, you would say, "____ ____ ____ ____ ____ ____."

names, persons, etc.

I 94.   After you have made your nomination, there would be no need for anyone to ____ the nomination.

I nominate Jane Smith for secretary.

I 95.   When the president decides that all of the nominations have been made, he will declare the nominations closed. After this no one can make a ____.

second

I 96.   If a member of the group would like
to close the nominations, he may do so by
saying, "I move that the ____ be closed." This
motion requires a second and vote.

nomination

I 97.   There are two ways to close the nominations. One is for the president to declare
____ ____ ____.

nominations

I 98.   The second way to close the nominations is for a member of the group to move
that the ____ ____ ____.

*the nominations
closed*

I 99.   The voting in elections may be done
any way the organization sees fit. Usually the
members wish to wait until all the names have
been ____ before voting.

*nominations be
closed*

I 100.   When the voting is by *ballot*, the president must wait until all the nominations have
been made so that the ____ can contain all
the names.

nominated

I 101.   In a ballot election—that is, when the
candidates are voted on by using a written ballot—the voters are NOT restricted to the ____
on the ballot but may write in other names.

ballot

I 102.   Candidates' names may not be written
in on the ballot if the organization's constitution and by-laws forbid this practice. If there
is no such restriction, then any member may
____ ____ a name or names for office.

candidates or names

I 103.   Write-in candidates can only be
counted when an organization votes by ballot
and the ____ and by-laws do not restrict such
practice.

write in

I 104.   A simple majority vote is required to elect the officers unless the organization's _____ and by-laws state otherwise.

constitution

I 105.   The vote required to elect officers is usually a _____ _____. In some cases the _____ _____ will state that another vote is required.

constitution

I 106.   If the constitution and by-laws state that a special procedure (or vote) will be followed in the elections, then that procedure must be followed. The *procedures* set forth in the constitution and by-laws take priority over all other _____.

simple majority · constitution and by-laws

I 107.   Review the material in this set by completing the following statements:
1. It is the duty of the _____ to announce the steps in the order of business as they come due in the meeting.
2. The _____ is responsible for all the records of the organization.
3. The exact procedure for the election of officers will be found in the organization's _____ _____ _____.
4. Unless otherwise specified in the constitution and by-laws, a _____ _____ vote is required to elect the officers.

procedures

You are now ready to begin Set J, Constitution and By-laws.

1) chairman 2) secretary 3) constitution and by-laws 4) simple majority

set J

CONSTITUTION AND BY-LAWS[1]

Place a card or piece of paper (approximately 3″ x 5″) over the page. Move the card down the page to expose one frame at a time. Read the frame carefully. The blanks in the frame indicate where essential information is missing; the number of blanks indicates the number of words in the desired response. Do not write in the blanks; write your response in the space to the right of the frame. Then move the card down to expose the next frame; as you do so you will also expose the correct answer to the previous frame, which is given in the right-hand column opposite the next frame. Check your answer before continuing the program.

J 1.   In forming an organization, there are recommended procedures to follow which will allow those people who are interested to _____ a group.

J 2.   First, discuss with others the idea of forming a club or organization, for a particular purpose and see if a majority would want to _____ such a group.

form or organize

J 3.   If you find that a majority would be interested in joining, then agree on a time and _____ to hold the first meeting.

form or join

J 4.   When the time arrives (it is customary to delay beginning the initial meeting fifteen or twenty minutes to be sure everyone interested has arrived), have the person most interested call the meeting to _____.

place

[1] For a more detailed discussion of this subject, see *Robert's Rules of Order Newly Revised*, pages 474-498.

J 5.   The first item to dispose of is the election of a temporary chairman (president). This person, when elected, is called the _____ pro tempore.

order

J 6.   The chairman *pro tempore*, when elected, will assume the duties of the chair and proceed to the election of a secretary _____ _____.

chairman or president

J 7.   The secretary pro tempore will, after elected, assume the duties of the _____.

pro tempore

J 8.   The next item on the agenda is a discussion of the purpose of organizing the group. After this has been agreed upon, someone should make a motion (or resolution) to _____ the group.

secretary

J 9.   The final item to dispose of at the first meeting is the appointment or election of a group to draw up a proposed _____ and by-laws for the group which will be presented at the next meeting.

organize

J 10.   The group drawing up the constitution and by-laws would NOT be a *committee* because "_____" is a technical term that is not used until the constitution is approved and the club is official.

constitution

J 11.   When this is finished, the chairman pro tempore will entertain a motion to _____ and thus end the meeting.

committee

J 12.   At the end of the first meeting, a time and place for the second meeting could be set by using the motion to fix _____ _____ _____ _____ _____ _____.

adjourn

J 13.   Sufficient time should be allowed between the first and second meetings so that
the group drawing up the ____ ____ ____
will be able to complete their task.

the time of the next meeting

J 14.   At the second meeting, the chairman
pro tempore and the secretary ____ ____ will
again assume their assigned duties.

constitution and by-laws

J 15.   The chairman pro tempore will call the
meeting to order; the secretary pro tempore
will read the minutes of the last meeting and
have the members ____ the minutes (as corrected).

pro tempore

J 16.   The chairman pro tempore will then
call for a report from the group drawing up
the ____ and by-laws.

approve

J 17.   Once the constitution and by-laws has
been adopted by the members, the election of
permanent ____ will follow.

constitution

J 18.   Once the permanent officers have been
elected, the permanent president (chairman)
will take over immediately, and the permanent
____ will take over immediately after their
election.

officers

J 19.   After the permanent president (chairman) has taken over, the group will continue
in the regular order of ____.

secretary

J 20.   The group appointed or nominated to
draw up a ____ and by-laws usually follows a
recommended outline of articles.

business

J 21.   These articles are the ones normally included in the constitution and by-laws when they are combined into a single document. Other documents could take precedence over an individual organization's ＿＿ and by-laws—for example, articles of incorporation, state and federal constitutions, etc.

constitution

J 22.   Although not a common practice, a constitution and by-laws could be drawn up by a group before the ＿＿ is formed.

constitution

J 23.   To make sure everything essential is covered in the ＿＿ and ＿＿ that is drawn up, the group must follow some kind of outline.

organization or club

J 24.   This outline is composed of articles, each of which is an important point to be covered in the ＿＿ and ＿＿.

constitution · by-laws

J 25.   A constitution and by-laws is composed of an ＿＿ which contains points called ＿＿.

constitution · by-laws

J 26.   There are usually seven of these points or ＿＿ in a constitution and by-laws. (See *Robert's Rules of Order Newly Revised*, pp. 10-12, for a slightly different set of articles. Use the set most appropriate for your organization.)

outline · articles

J 27.   How many articles are usually found in a constitution and by-laws?

articles

J 28.   The first article included is the *name*. The organization's name is simply stated as a matter of record to designate that this constitution refers to the organization carrying this ＿＿.

seven

J 29.   The second article is *purposes.* This article presents a general statement of the objectives of the organization and how these _____ are to be attained.

name

J 30.   After the name and the purposes, the third article is *membership.* This article includes such items as the qualifications of members, the method of selection, the classes of members, and the amount of dues to be paid by _____.

purposes or objectives

J 31.   What are the first three articles included in a constitution and by-laws? List them.

members

J 32.   The fourth article is *officers.* This article designates the names and duties of each _____ in the organization.

1) name 2) purposes 3) membership

J 33.   Article one of the constitution and by-laws is name; article two is _____; article three is membership; article four is _____.

officer

J 34.   The fifth article is *committees.* This article lists the standing committees and their duties as well as the procedure for forming special _____.

purposes · officers

J 35.   The sixth article, called *meetings,* includes the frequency of meetings and the procedure for calling special _____.

committees

J 36.   The definition of a quorum is included under the heading of meetings in article number _____.

meetings

J 37.   A quorum is the minimum number of club members necessary to transact business.

six

The quorum is designated under article number _____ of the _____ _____ _____.

J 38. The seventh and last article usually
found in the constitution and by-laws is called
amendment. This article states the vote required to _____ the constitution and by-laws.

*six · constitution
and by-laws*

J 39. Article seven should also specify the
method by which the constitution can be
amended, such as prior notice to all members
of the intention to _____ the constitution.

amend

J 40. This prior notice of amending the constitution can have several forms—circulation
of the amendment, written notice of the proposed amendment, or simply a notice that an
_____ will be proposed to the constitution.

amend

J 41. Fill in the missing articles and study
the others:
1.
2.
3. membership
4. officers
5. committees
6. meetings
7.

amendment

J 42. Again fill in the missing articles and
study the others:
1. name
2. purposes
3.
4.
5. committees
6.
7. amendment

*1) name 2) purposes
7) amendment*

J 43. Now list all *seven* articles usually included in a constitution and by-laws.

*3) membership
4) officers
6) meetings*

J 44.   The organization's constitution and by-laws becomes the basic document of the organization and the supreme authority governing the members of the ____.

1) name 2) purposes 3) membership 4) officers 5) committees 6) meetings 7) amendment

J 45.   The basic document called the ____ and ____ is the supreme authority for an organization.

organization

J 46.   The basic document called the constitution and by-laws is the supreme ____ for an organization.

constitution · by-laws

J 47.   Although the constitution and by-laws is the ____ authority, the organization needs a code or manual of parliamentary procedure to regulate its regular business meetings.

authority

J 48.   The most popular manual is probably *Robert's Rules of Order Newly Revised.* This book is used as a reference and as a supplement to the supreme authority which is the ____ ____ ____.

supreme

J 49.   The most commonly used reference manual for parliamentary procedure is ____ ____ ____ ____ ____.

constitution and by-laws

J 50.   Although *Robert's Rules of Order Newly Revised* is used as a reference manual, the supreme and final ____ for procedure and rules is the constitution and by-laws.

Robert's Rules of Order Newly Revised

J 51.   From what you have learned, complete the following statements:
1. The constitution and by-laws is the supreme ____ for an organization.
2. The most commonly used reference manual

authority

for parliamentary procedure is ⎯⎯ ⎯⎯
⎯⎯ ⎯⎯ ⎯⎯ ⎯⎯.

You have now completed the final set in this
program.

*1) authority or docu-
ment 2) Robert's
Rules of Order New-
ly Revised*

A FINAL REVIEW OF PARLIAMENTARY PROCEDURE

1. Where does the term "parliamentary procedure" come from?

2. List the steps in the order of business.

3. What is the procedure for gaining the floor in a meeting?

4. List the three ways in which a motion may be amended.

5. What is an amendment to the main motion called? What is an amendment to the amendment called?

6. What is a simple majority vote?

7. What is the simplest way to determine a two-thirds majority?

8. Number the following motions in their order of precedence.
   _____Amend
   _____Lay on the table
   _____Adjourn
   _____Previous question
   _____Limit debate
   _____Recess
   _____Main motion proposing some new action
   _____Postpone indefinitely
   _____Question of privilege
   _____Fix the time of the next meeting
   _____Committee of the whole

9. What motion would you use to:
   a. Find out the proper procedure to make a motion.

   b. Defend yourself against a personal attack.

c. Correct an error in procedure.

d. Override a ruling by the chair.

e. Gain information concerning pending business.

f. Nullify a motion passed at a previous meeting.

g. Dispose of another member's motion without voting on it after debate has begun.

h. Test the voting strength without actually voting on the relevant question.

i. Check the results of a voice vote.

j. Change your vote from "yes" to "no" on a motion just passed.

10. Write *P* for privileged motions, *S* for subsidiary motions, *M* for main motions, and *I* for incidental motions.

_____Previous question
_____Orders of the day
_____Object to consideration
_____Postpone indefinitely
_____Lay on the table
_____Take from the table
_____Suspend the rules
_____Postpone definitely
_____Withdraw a motion
_____Refer to a committee
_____Special order of business

11. What special qualifications must be met by a person moving to reconsider?

12. Name the two types of committees and explain how they differ.

13. Mark *T* for true and *F* for false.

_____Parliamentary procedure must be exactly the same for all organizations.

_____It is possible to change or rephrase another member's motion without amending it.

_____The chairman can take an active part in the meeting and voice his views at any time.

_____A motion that is laid on the table will automatically be brought up and voted on at the next meeting.

_____If the chairman is not sure what ruling to make, the safest thing for him to do is to call for a vote.

14. When can the chairman vote?

15. What book is the best reference manual on parliamentary procedure?

16. What is the final and supreme authority governing an organization?

17. List the articles commonly found in a combined constitution and by-laws.

Appendix

SUGGESTED STUDY OUTLINES

OBJECTIVES

1. An understanding of the basic essentials of parliamentary procedure.
2. An awareness of the theory and practice of good parliamentary procedure.
3. A knowledge of the correct procedures to use in meetings.
4. Poise in administering the various offices of an organization.
5. Better participation as a member in an organization.

CLASS STUDY OUTLINE

1. Explain the general procedure to follow in using *Parliamentary Procedure: A Programmed Introduction, Revised Edition.*
2. Designate a time for the completion of the program, but let the students proceed through the program at their own rate. (Average time is five hours.)
3. Have the students complete the Final Review of Parliamentary Procedure, page 122.
4. Organize laboratory club meetings.
   a. Draw up constitution and by-laws (See Sample Constitution and By-laws for Classroom Use), page 127.
   b. Assign students to the various offices and committees outlined in the Sample Constitution and By-laws.
   c. Introduce *Robert's Rules of Order Newly Revised* as parliamentary authority and explain how it should be used.
5. Practice parliamentary procedure in laboratory club meetings. Change officers and have the committees report as outlined in the Roster of Officers, page 129.
6. Hold critique sessions.
   a. Discuss the strategy used by various students in the meetings and review special problems encountered. Emphasize how various motions can be used to increase or decrease the efficiency of an organization.

b. Assign students to create certain problem situations at the laboratory meeting and then at the following critique session discuss the procedure used.
7. Maintain a permanent record of the minutes and committee reports. Check the minutes periodically to see whether their form and content are correct.
8. Assign students to give critiques of the business meetings of various campus organizations.

INDIVIDUAL STUDY OUTLINE

1. Complete the entire program, *Parliamentary Procedure: A Programmed Introduction, Revised Edition.* Be sure to read the Instructions carefully before you start the program.
2. Keep a record of your answers so that you can review particular problems later in *Robert's Rules of Order Newly Revised.*
3. Use *Robert's Rules of Order Newly Revised* to familiarize yourself with all phases of parliamentary procedure.
4. Accept every opportunity to participate in business meetings either as a member or as an officer.

SAMPLE CONSTITUTION AND BY-LAWS FOR CLASSROOM USE
(Classes might like to organize a Parliamentary Law Club)

CONSTITUTION OF _____

I. *Name of the Organization*
The name of the organization shall be _____ .

II. *The Purpose of the Organization*
A. General statement of objectives
B. Means of attaining objectives

II. *Membership*
All students in _____ (name of course)
shall be members of this club.

V. *Officers*
A. The officers shall be as follows:
  1. Chairman
  2. Parliamentarian
  3. Secretary
B. The officers shall be appointed by the Roster of Officers.
C. The officers' duties:
  1. The chairman shall:
    a. Call the meeting to order on time and proceed with the usual order of business if a quorum is present.
    b. Maintain order in the meeting at all times—one motion and one speaker at a time.
    c. Decide all parliamentary questions with the advice of the parliamentarian.
    d. Preside impartially and impersonally—even referring to himself as "the chair."
    e. State each motion after it has been seconded and before opening debate. After debate, restate the motion before taking the vote. Announce the results after each vote has been taken.
    f. If he wishes to speak, let the parliamentarian take over the chair.
  2. The parliamentarian shall:
    a. Act as an advisor to the chairman on all questions of parliamentary procedure.
    b. Be constantly alert for errors in procedure.
    c. Give a report at the end of each meeting.
  3. The secretary shall:
    a. Keep a roll of all members.
    b. Keep a record of all committee members.
    c. Keep minutes of all meetings.
    d. Have a copy of the constitution and by-laws with him at all meetings.
    e. Assist the chairman when called upon.

V. *Committees*
   A. Standing Committees: (Divide the organization into work groups and designate a committee name for each one, followed by a description of the committee's duties.)

   1. _____

   2. _____

   3. _____

   4. _____

   5. _____

   6. _____

   B. Special committees shall be appointed by the chairman or by a motion from the floor.

VI. *Meetings*
   A. The meetings shall be held _____ (days and hour).
   B. Special meetings shall be called by the instructor.
   C. A quorum shall be _____ .
   D. The parliamentary authority shall be *Robert's Rules of Order Newly Revised.*

VII. *Amendments*
   A. Voting on proposed amendments to the constitution must take place on the first regular meeting after the amendment has been proposed. Discussion is in order at both meetings.
   B. The vote required to change the constitution is set at _____ of the membership.

ROSTER OF OFFICERS

This roster is designed for twenty members and ten meetings.

List the members in alphabetical order:

1. _____ 11. _____

2. _____ 12. _____

3. _____ 13. _____

4. _____ 14. _____

5. _____ 15. _____

6. _____ 16. _____

7. _____ 17. _____

8. _____ 18. _____

9. _____ 19. _____

10. _____ 20. _____

The officers at each meeting will be:

Meeting	Chairman	Parliamentarian	Secretary
I	1	2	4
II	9	5	7
III	3	19	12
IV	11	8	16
V	20	4	17
VI	12	18	13
VII	14	7	2
VIII	10	13	18
IX	17	15	19
X	16	6	1

In case of the absence of any officer, the member who most recently held that office will fill in. The secretary is responsible for passing on the minutes (in final form) to the new secretary.

SUGGESTED OUTLINE FOR MINUTES

The minutes are easier to use as a reference if prepared in outline form. Be sure to include:
1. Name of the organization.
2. Date, hour, place, and kind of meeting.
3. Names of regular chairman and secretary if they were present or names of their substitutes.
4. Each main motion and the name of the person making it. State whether the motion passed or failed and give the vote on the question.
5. Whether the minutes of the previous meeting were read and approved—as read or as corrected.
6. All points of order and appeals whether sustained or lost along with the chairman's reasons for the ruling.
7. Special motions which might be of concern and/or interest in future meetings (at discretion of secretary).
8. Time and method of adjournment.
9. Signature of the secretary.

Do not summarize the discussion which took place at the meeting or make value judgments about events transpiring during the meeting. You may include a brief summary of committee reports instead of placing the entire report in the minutes. (See *Robert's Rules of Order Newly Revised*, pages 389- 392.)

SAMPLE COMMITTEE REPORT

December 20

FROM: The Membership Committee

TO: The University Parliamentary Law Club

The Membership Committee wishes to report that the club as of last week has a total membership of 200. This figure represents a 10% increase over last year's membership. Since this is this largest percentage of growth shown by the organization in the past 10 years, the committee recommends the following:

1. The annual membership drive in November be continued for two more years.

2. The dues not be raised for at least one more year.

3. The members be encouraged to seek new members in order to strengthen our organization.

Submitted by:

John McConnell, Chairman
Polly Gray
Aylean Crouse

GLOSSARY OF MOTIONS

(Numbers in parentheses refer to pages in *Robert's Rules of Order Newly Revised* on which a detailed discussion of the particular motion may be found.)

1. Adjourn - To close the meeting (199-207).
2. Amend - To propose a change or modification in a main motion (108-140).
3. Appeal from the decision of the chair - To appeal to the assembly to override a ruling made by the chair (213-214, 218-222).
4. Committee of the whole - To consider a motion informally, using group discussion methods (442-450).
5. Division of the assembly - To ask for a re-vote by means which would produce a readily distinguishable division between "yes" and "no" votes. (237-239).
6. Fix the time to which to adjourn - To set a time for reassembling (207-211).
7. Lay on the table - To postpone consideration of a question temporarily (177-185, 253-254, 322-323).
8. Limit debate - To restrict the time or number of speakers for debate on a motion (161-166).
9. Main motion - To propose action concerning the general business of an organization (46-47, 82-104).
10. Special order of business - To set a specific time for the exclusive consideration of a particular question (309-311).
11. Object to consideration - To object to the consideration of a motion considered irrelevant or objectionable (227-229, 423-424).
12. Orders of the day - To request that the group conform to the order of business (186-191).
13. Parliamentary inquiry - To seek advice from the chair concerning parliamentary procedure (245).
14. Point of information - To request information concerning pending business (245-246).
15. Point of order - To call attention to an error in parliamentary procedure (212-218).
16. Postpone indefinitely - To dispose of a motion without voting upon it (105-108).
17. Postpone to a certain time - To delay until a specified time any action upon a pending question (150-161).
18. Previous question - To terminate discussion on a debatable motion by bringing it to an immediate vote (166-177).
19. Question of privilege - A request for the chair to deal with an emergency situation (191-196).
20. Recess - To temporarily disband for a specific purpose (196-199).
21. Reconsider - To give the group an opportunity to consider again a vote already taken (265-281).

22. Refer or commit - To delay action or investigate further a question by referring it to a committee (140-150).
23. Rescind - To cancel an action taken at a previous meeting (256-260).
24. Suspend the rules - To make possible for a temporary period a procedure contrary to the standing rules (222-227).
25. Take from the table or Resume consideration - To revive a motion previously laid on the table, or temporarily put aside (180-181).
26. Withdraw a motion - To prevent action on a motion when the maker of the motion has changed his mind   (246-248).